Clean Your Plate!

13 Things Good Parents Say that Ruin Kids' Lives

Liz Bayardelle, Ph.D.

For information, contact
MSI Press
1760-F Airline Highway, #203
Hollister, CA 95023

Cover design & layout: Carl Leaver

Cover art: Annie Zweizig

Copyeditor: Betty Lou Leaver

LCCN: 2020918224

ISBN: 978-1-950328-79-6

Dedication

This book would not have been possible without three groups of very special people:

- Julie and Tom: the amazing parents who raised me to (mostly) functional adulthood
- Natalie, Tyson, and Kayla: the kids who inspire, perplex, enchant, and motivate me
- Anthony: the incredible husband without whom my family, sanity, and life in general would simply not exist

Finally, this book is also dedicated to all the smart, ambitious, exhausted, marker-stained, and incredibly committed parents out there. Your parenting efforts may be unseen or underappreciated in the short-term, but they will be hugely appreciated in the long term.

Just keep swimming.

Liz Bayardelle, Ph.D.

Contents

Liz Bayardelle, Ph.D.

Introduction

Parenting is hard.

It's not "I would rather be hiding state secrets in a POW camp" hard, but it's definitely "my most cherished fantasy is about taking an uninterrupted shower by myself" hard. It's hard because you are a parent 24/7 without coffee breaks or vacations. It's hard because it isolates you away from your friends, sometimes your family, and occasionally any semblance of adult human companionship whatsoever. It's hard because you always put the needs of others above your own, often without thanks or even acknowledgement. (If all three of these statements are true at the same time, it's called "having an infant.")

Even worse, not only is parenting diabolically challenging, but it also has the outside appearance of being easy, fun, and less challenging than a "real" job.

Yes, many non-parents attempt to compare the act of childrearing to any other job. However, until they find a job where it is impossible to quit, you aren't paid, and your boss is allowed to wake you up at 3 a.m. by *And the ribs. That wasn't in the employee handbook.* [Crystal] repeatedly kicking you in the face[1], I would like to heartily request that they kindly mind their own biscuits.

Despite all of this, the very hardest thing about parenting is that you love your kids more than literally anything else in the world, so almost every choice you make as a parent is accompanied by a crippling fear that you aren't doing well enough by your kids.

You want to be the most fun parent ever so that they get the most out of their childhoods, but you also have to be strict enough that they learn discipline, respect, and priorities. You want to buy them everything under the sun, but you also want

---

1   If you don't understand this last one, don't worry; you have just clearly never slept next to a toddler.

1

to teach them to earn their own way. You want to let them learn to make their own choices, but you would happily throw that awful new kid they just started hanging out with off the nearest cliff if you were certain enough you could do it without getting caught.

Yes, welcome to parenting.

As a parent, you now have the unhappy pleasure of second guessing every statement that comes out of your mouth because you so badly want to be a perfect parent for the kids you love more than life itself.

This book is aimed at helping you dissect the pros and cons of some of the most common parental statements. Its purpose is to give you more research to back up your parental decisions, to bring to life some of the common pitfalls of these frequently-spouted phrases, and make you snort-laugh (hopefully in public) at least once along the way.

What This Book Is

The "ruin their lives" part of the title is simply a humorous way of saying that even some of the most well-intentioned advice can backfire.

These backfires can be due to age-old wisdom not standing the test of time, the fact that often parental advice comes more from our own fear than anything else, that something gets lost in translation, or merely because kids often hear whatever they want to hear (if they're even listening at all).

No matter the reason, it's important we think through the things we drill into our kids' heads.

I can tell you first-hand that, as a 30-something woman with three kids of my own, I still hear my mother's voice in my head when I do (or don't do) certain things. We parents are a huge part of who our kids will grow up to be so it's a good idea to take the time to think through the words they'll probably still hear in their heads, even as adults, every time they forget to pick up their socks.

With this in mind, an alternative name for this book could have been *The Overthinker's Guide to Parental Advice*.

Basically, you're in for an in-depth look at a lot of the expressions our kids hear coming out of our mouths (often with the same frequency as swear words at a Raiders' game).

As You Read This Book

First and foremost, I hope you get a kick out of this book. We parents have little spare time so if you're choosing to spend your precious "me time" reading this, the least I can do is make you giggle embarrassingly to yourself while stand-

If a mother giggles alone, does it make a sound? [Crystal]

ing the middle of the grocery store aisle (because we all know you're not actually reading this sitting down in a quiet room).

Second, the purpose of this book is to help bring up some of the important grey area points of contention in these common statements. I'm not actually advocating stopping saying most of these things, but if you have already considered the research, questionable interpretations, and problems behind each of these common parent-isms, then you're more likely to say them in a way that helps your kids (instead of scarring them for life...no pressure).

Finally, some of these I consider to be legitimately necessary Public Service Announcements (like Chapter 4, for example). If my writing this can save even one toddler from being forced to kiss the cheek of their inebriated uncle or perfume-wafting aunt at a holiday gathering, then I've done my job as a human being and can go to bed happy. (Ha, ha! Like my kids let me sleep!)

Most of these chapters are standalone enough for you to skip around. However, I do refer back to things every once in a while so if you don't have a pressing need to skip to a later chapter, it might make for a more seamless reading experience if you go through the chapters in order.

Skimmer's Tips: The Basic Structure

For those of you who tend to skip around and skim, let me make your life easier.

> *Or if you're so exhausted you can't form complete thoughts.* [Kristine]

Each chapter follows the same basic structure:

- **Title:** This is the thing you say that is going to (hypothetically) ruin your kid's life.

- **Doctor's Warning:** Just like prescription drugs have an intended use and a whole load of unwanted side effects,[2] these parental sayings have what you want to convey to your kids and what message you actually end up sending. This doctor's warning stamp is a basic summary of how things could go terribly, terribly wrong. This is great if you want the uber-short version of a chapter in just a few minutes. Just don't operate heavy machinery afterward.

- **Why We Say It:** Each of these sayings is common for a reason. Yes, the premise of this book is that you're ruining your kids' lives...but you still have a point! This section covers the actual objective of each phrase we discuss.

---

2   Nausea, cramps, growing a leathery tail, male pattern baldness, not being able to open your eyes on days with more than two syllables, an irresistible urge to sing the Cambodian national anthem whenever you see a red car, etc.

- **Research Says (What They Hear):** This part is a research-based explanation of the message your kids are actually getting when they hear these words come out of your mouth. This is an empirically-backed summary of how a well-intentioned message can go very far off the tracks.

- **What to Say Instead:** Most of these things are, as you can guess, based on messages you absolutely should convey to your children (despite the title). The problems lie in the delivery. This section will help you refine that delivery and sidestep as many of the potential issues as possible.

- **Cheat Sheet:** This section takes into account everything discussed throughout the entire chapter and gives you clear, tangible, bullet-form, hands-on advice about how to convey the desired message without any of the undesirable side effects.

Parenting: Now a Team Sport

Before I let you get to it, I want to address one more key problem with our current model of parenting: isolation.

One of the biggest problems new parents (actually all parents) face is that your social network is forcibly ripped away from you just when you need social support the most. That's why you end up rocking a sleepless baby aimlessly around Costco at 6:15am, looking like a homeless person, wearing several varieties of bodily fluid stains on your shirt, and muttering to yourself in full sentences about cheese.

Or driving aimlessly around the streets at 3am. [Kristine]

We parents have to focus all our time on our kids, but this has the unfortunate side effect of depriving us of adult social contact. Well, it's more that the luxury adult conversation is forcibly ripped from you by a screaming baby seemingly hell-bent on turning your life into a psychology experiment on sleep deprivation.

The last thing you need as a parent is another person telling you all the things you should be doing better as you fumble your way through trying to raise functional children. So, given every parent's deep-seated desire to just talk to another adult human for a few minutes without being shouted at, punched, or asked for a snack, I thought it might be nice for this book to come with a built-in network of sarcastic parents. Consider them your imaginary friends. (Goodness knows, I do.)

The following two women are real parents of real (loud) kids. As you read the book, you'll not only get my perspective as the step-mom of a teenage girl and the bio-mom of a 4-year-old and a 6-month-old, you'll also get the perspectives of a few other (equally sarcastic) parents of different pack configurations.

As you have probably noticed, as you read you'll occasionally see little comments in the margins, a "mommentary" if you will. These are the comments of other real life parents just as sleep-deprived as you are. Meet the team:

Crystal, Adoptive Mom of a 4-Year-Old Ninja

Crystal is the adoptive mom of a 4-year-old boy who will most likely be a Navy SEAL or civil engineer (or both). Her hobbies include not sleeping, binge stress-cleaning, and hiding behind the sofa to consume chocolate. Her adult human persona (outside of being a mom, if such a thing exists) is an interior designer by day (inspiredhaven.com) and a mom blogger by night (designfulmama.com). Multi-tasking much?

Kristine, Mom of a 5-Year-Old and a Toddlernado

Kristine generally spends her days trying to keep her two little people alive, keep her businesses running (with screaming in the background), and keep her sanity in check through much needed consulting (otherwise known as therapy). Her motto is that parenthood is a guessing game with a million handbooks. In "real life," she's a blogger (KrisBeeMama.com), WordPress website creator (KitBlogs.com), doer of all the things, and a self-proclaimed Chaos Coordinator (Can you tell?).

How It Works

These real-life moms went through an early draft of this book and, as you can predict, had some pretty hilarious comments, questions, and stories as they read. I felt immensely selfish keeping these witticisms for just myself, so you get to team read the book with your tribe of imaginary friends. Just pretend you're sitting at a coffee house (or more likely in the viewing room of a preschool gymnastics class), talking to other adults that were similarly crazy enough to procreate.

With that being said, I'll leave you to it. Happy reading!

Liz Bayardelle, Ph.D.

Do You Need Any Money?

Intended Use: To make sure your kid earns enough money to make it back from wherever they're going without hitch hiking or going hungry

Possible Side Effects: Destroying intrinsic motivation, reduced financial skills, and decreased success in future vocational, social, interpersonal, and emotional skills

The trope of Mom or Dad being a child's ATM has gotten so common it's not even a funny Internet meme anymore. (And if you're at all familiar with the Internet, that's really saying something.) Every parent knows that it's probably bad just to hand their kid money whenever they want something, but that doesn't mean we're actually good at resisting the urge to do just that when the situation arises.

Why We Say It

If it helps assuage your parental guilt at all, this isn't a bad impulse to have. You've spent the entirety of your child's life trying to provide for all their needs, even trying to anticipate your child's needs before they even occur so your little

Why yes. Yes, I do. In fact. [Crystal]

kidlet doesn't have to want for anything. Do any of you moms out there have a purse whose sheer heft equals your body weight due to the abundance of granola bars, spare socks, and just in case toys?[3]

It's because you want to make sure your kid has everything they need at all times.

While this impulse can make you a fantastic parent, it's also the thing that, when applied to the financial realm, is going to turn your kid into a spoiled little freeloader.

Research Says (What They Hear)

I'm not going to tell parents never to give their kids money because not only would that be incredibly unrealistic it would also be entirely hypocritical. However, I do want to convey that the way you handle the issue of money with your kids can have a serious, measurable, and long-term effect on how they handle, think about, and relate to money for the rest of their lives.

My kiddo thinks we acquire things by magic. Money? [Crystal]

Childhood Should Prepare You for the Real World

The first thing I want to stress here is that whatever financial system you choose to adopt with your kids, it should be geared toward preparing them for adulthood.

Is 6 too young? He's kind of a mature 4. [Crystal]

When they turn 18 (or 21, or 35, or whatever age at which you choose to release them into the wild), they will enter the "real world" armed only with the knowledge you gave them and the habits you repeatedly drilled into their heads.

If you give them money with no strings attached any time they want anything, there's a solid chance that they'll enter the adult world expecting roughly the same treatment. Unfortunately, this usually means that their outstretched palm will somehow eventually end up pointing back in your direction as there aren't very many employers willing to dole out high salaries for no work.[4]

What To Say Instead

So, keeping in mind this horror story of your future 45-year-olds still looking to you when they want to buy a car, let's delve into why kids need money, the different

---

3   Yes, I do literally carry around an "emergency soccer ball" in my purse. It's saved my parental neck on more than one occasion. Parenthood pulls no punches.

4   Trust me, I googled it.

ways you can give it to them, and what message each of these different methods is going to send to their developing ideas of how the world works.

Why Kids Do Actually Need Spending Money

If you're anything like me, you've probably wondered why exactly kids need money when we're the ones who buy their clothes, food, rent, toys, and basically everything else. The short answer is that they really don't need money right now, but they desperately need a safe environment for practicing their financial skills so they don't end up in the poor house later.

Childhood is the time when you introduce your kid to important financial concepts that they'll need later in life. This list includes (but is definitely not limited to) things like:

- how to budget their expenses (or their wants) against a regularly occurring, fixed amount (i.e. a salary or allowance);

- how to save money over time for a desired purchase that is larger than the amount of money you currently have;

- how to find ways to earn extra money when you have higher expenses than usual;

- the fact that you don't need to spend all of your money the second you earn it; and/or

- how to give a portion of your money to charity

As you can see, this is a pretty important list of skills for your kiddo to learn.

That's why it's important that they practice their financial skills with money and expenses that don't really matter while they still have you as a safety net.

If they're 12 and accidentally blow their entire savings on Legos so they don't have enough money to go to the movies with their friends, they will feel temporary discomfort, but it won't be the end of the world. If they don't learn how to budget, save, and spend wisely, they could be 30 and blow all their money on a big-screen television so they don't have enough money to pay rent.

Nope. Mine hoards it like a squirrel... [Kristine]

You want them to make their mistakes (and learn from them) when the stakes are small and they have you as a backup so that they don't make them later when the stakes are higher. So, while you do pay for rent, food, clothes, school, and basically everything else that matters, it's still important for your kids to have a way of earning, saving, and spending their own money because it gives them a nice, low-pressure laboratory to simulate what it'll be like in the big scary world.

So, How Do Kids Get Money?

So, now that we can all agree kids need some kind of financial experience, the questions become how do we give them money, how much should they get, and what (if any) rules should be attached to the way they spend it?

We'll go over each of these questions in the upcoming sections, but before we go any further, I want to make one thing very clear: not all household chores should be paid.

The Case for Unpaid Chores

There is a wealth of psychological research that demonstrates the long-term benefits of having kids do chores. Kids who were given chores at home have been shown to have better social relationships and higher grades, get better early-career jobs, and manifest a higher degree of self-sufficiency (M. Rossman, 2002, cited in Wallace, 2015). These findings were strongest for kids who started chores early (around the ages of 3 or 4) but still existed even for those who started chores as teenagers.

The reason these chores were so important is that they taught children how to be a member of an ecosystem, assess their surroundings for what needs to be done, and then help out by taking care of it.

I couldn't agree more! [Crystal]

If you think about this skill set in the context of a friendship, romantic relationship, or work environment, it is no surprise that kids who develop these skills by helping out around the house would be more successful later in life.

As if all the benefits of having them do chores without compensation weren't enough to convince you that you shouldn't bribe, pay, or otherwise financially motivate your kids to do their chores, there are also some serious downsides to the act of paying your kid to do their chores which might just swing you.

Dangers of Paid Chores

It's important to note that the benefits described above disappear when children are financially compensated for doing those chores. Yes, you read that right. If you pay your kids for doing something,

And will also completely backfire when I fold first. [Crystal]

you are actually making it less likely that they will ever do that thing again...unless you continue paying them to do it.

Think of it this way. By paying a child for a chore, you're sending their little mind the subliminal message "this task is so unpleasant that you would never voluntarily do it so I'm going to make it worth your while with this here fiver".

On the other hand, if you have your kids do chores without financial compensation, other forms of bribery, or punishment if the chores go undone, you're sending the message, "Yes, this might not be the most fun way to spend a Saturday, but we're all members of this family so you are expected to pitch in."

I want to bring up an important psychological concept here: intrinsic motivation. Intrinsic motivation is the desire to do something for your own, personal satisfaction rather than because someone told (or paid, bribed, or blackmailed) you to do it. This applies strongly to the concept of chores because a majority of a kid's chores are things we eventually want them to be able to do of their own volition[5].

A great deal of psychological research has been done on the subject (Deci & Ryan, 2015), and the consensus is clear: paying a child to do something is the absolute fastest way to kill their intrinsic motivation to ever do that thing again. This is why it's so important to have a base of unpaid chores that have to be done nonetheless to have your kid help out as a productive member of the family.

So, What About Paid Chores?

But wait, you say, this section started with a discussion of how necessary it was for kids to have access to money in order to build their burgeoning financial savvy. What's the catch?

This is where it gets complicated, because both of these completely contradictory facts are true:

You should not pay children for doing their fair share of household chores.

It's important for kids to get paid for chores in order to learn essential financial skills.

These statements seem to conflict, but it is indeed possible to do both of these things at the same time. You just need to get a little creative with your system. In the next section, we'll go over how to create a financial system that will dodge all the potential ways you can turn your kid into a lazy freeloader while accruing all the benefits of chores and allowances.[6]

The Anatomy of a Chore Chart

In my humble (yet well researched) opinion, there are four main components to any good chores system. Each of the following parts has a practical, real-world-oriented purpose that should teach your kids a specific set of skills they'll need later in life.[7]

Part 1: Mandatory, Non-Paid Chores

Primary Goal: To teach your children that they are part of a family, and, as such, they have to pull their own weight without needing to be compensated for it.

---

5   You know, without us having to beg, blackmail, force, nag, swindle, plead, and bribe them to do it.

6   It'll be a bit like Neo dodging bullets in *The Matrix*. Get pumped.

7   If you want a printable version of this chore chart, you can download the free fillable/printable PDF from my blog at https://www.thestaysanemom.com/chores

Remember, these should be chores that serve the family, not just chores that serve the kid themself.

Real-World Equivalent: In the scary land of actual adulting, the degree of goodwill your children have with their boss, coworkers, or family will not be determined by what your children (by then full-fledged adults) are "required" to do. They will be good employees, spouses, or parents because of the things they do without compensation just to make their immediate surroundings better, happier places.

Sample Chores: These are usually "keeping the peace" and "doing their part" type chores, like keeping common rooms clean, clearing plates after dinner, or putting away laundry (older kids can fold or even wash as well). I wouldn't put anything too huge on this list, just enough chores that kids actually pull at least some of their own weight and help out as part of the family. Bonus: this can (and should) actually take some work off your plate.

Part 2: A Small, Flat-Fee Allowance Base

Primary Goal: To teach your kid how to manage money. This shouldn't be enough to buy anything significant (or they'll casually neglect their flat-fee chores [see Part 3] because they don't need the money), but it should be enough that you can use it to teach them the basics of saving, spending, and giving.

Real-World Equivalent: In real life, this won't really exist (because no one gets money for nothing), but childhood is a time to practice things they'll use later on. So, now is when they need to practice their future financial skills.

Sample Fee: This differs based on the child's age, but I'd give a loose guideline where you take 1/5th the price of an average toy. That way if the kid forgoes their paying chores (parts 3 and 4) completely, they'd have to save for five weeks to buy a toy. For a toddler, this would probably be $2 or $3. For a teenager, it might be $5 to $15.

Part 3: Mandatory, Flat-Fee Chores

Primary Goal: To teach your kid that there's a certain standard that has to be upheld in order for him/her to get a paycheck. This is not negotiable, and you can't split it up (aka no "you did 5 of 6 chores so you get 5/6 your allowance"). It's all or nothing.

Real-World Equivalent: This teaches your kids how it is to work for a salary. There's no haggling, and you have no say in it. You do 100% your job and get 100% of your paycheck. If your kids miss a chore you should act like a boss would: give them a warning, and if it happens again (or, with a three strikes policy, two more times) they get "fired" and don't get allowance that week. If you want to be really "authentic" with it, you can let them skip chores on special occasions (e.g. the night before a big test or the day of a long sporting event) if they give you written notice in advance, just like a boss would give leave upon employee request.

Sample Chores/Fee: Make sure the amount of chores is enough that they do something every day but not so much that they can't get it done on a normal home-work night. In our house, our 14-year-old has to fill up all the dog bowls (daily), do the dinner dishes, and keep her areas of the house clean. I'd probably have this weekly fee the same amount as one cheap-ish toy for the age group or 1/3 to 1/2 of one nicer toy for that age group.

Part 4: Optional, For-a-Fee Chores

Primary Goal: To give kids a way they can earn extra income when they have something they *really* want to buy. This is important because, as they ask for things, you can control their spending by making them earn it. Is your child begging for that shiny new *insert crazy, useless kid gizmo here*? Now you can just smile, say "you know what to do, kiddo," and hand over a mop.

Real-World Equivalent: This is similar to picking up some extra shifts at work, taking on more contract work, or other variable-fee jobs in the adult world.

Sample Chores/Fees: I'd make a "menu" for kids so they have a list of tasks to choose from, each with a differ-ent amount of money. This could be stuff like helping vacuum, clean-ing windows, folding laundry, emp-tying the dishwasher, walking the dogs, or basically anything that's age-appropriate.

Mine may quit preschool and take the vocational track. [Crystal]

This may be too much fun for my avid negotiator. [Kristine]

If you want to maximize real-world parallels, you can also add a "propose a task" option where they have to sug-gest the task and negotiate their fee for completing it.

Two Quick Caveats: Before you make your menu, keep these two, key points in mind. They might not make a huge difference now, but they'll play a huge psycho-logical impact on your kids later:

1. Don't put anything on this list that you ever want them to do for free again. It's very hard to turn a paying task into something they have to do for free.

2. Don't add anything here like reading, studying, or other tasks you want them to end up enjoying. Things on this list will be mentally filed under the "work" category, which is usually also named as the "things I don't enjoy doing" category. If you put reading on here, they'll end up with the impression that reading is something un-

pleasant that they need to be paid to do.[8] The "chores menu" should be comprised of things that are pretty universally "unfun" tasks like cleaning or other busywork.

The Need for Need

We've discussed the "supply" end of your kid's finances, but the "demand" side should also get a little bit of attention.

The point of having a financial system is to teach your kids how to manage their money as an adult, but they don't have those pesky expenses we have as adults. We grown-up folk go to work every day because without our salary we can't afford things like food or rent. This is a pretty significant motivator.

Or if you stay home because child care is sadistically expensive. [Kristine]

Unfortunately, there's no driving force quite so urgent in your child's financial ecosystem. No matter what chores they do (or don't do) you're going to pay for their food, housing, school, and other necessary expenses, so why bother taking the garbage out?

This is when the art of creating valid needs comes in. You never want to deprive your child of the necessities, but you do want them to have an actual need for things that they have to buy for themselves. Without the motivation of an actual need, they won't have much incentive to earn money for themselves and, consequently, won't learn the lessons they need to be learning.

That's where you come in. You can start small, especially if you have little kids. Make them pay for a portion of their own toys. Put them in charge of buying their own candy if they want an extra snack when you go to the grocery store.

Iccceeeee creeaaaammm! [Crystal]

You don't have to do anything too extreme, but take a tiny percentage of their "needs" and give it to them to pay for. Now, you want to make sure they have enough money to actually do so relatively consistently, so balance their total allowance amount with the total cost of the expenses for which they'll be expected to foot the bill.

As they get older you can gradually increase their scope of responsibilities (as well as their allowance) to match their growing level of responsibility. For example, while a toddler might only be able to be responsible to earn (and save) for extra pieces of candy at the supermarket checkout during your weekly grocery runs, an elementary schooler could reasonably be put in charge of their entire toy budget (i.e. "if you want the toy you can save up and pay for it"), a middle schooler could start paying for their nonessential clothing (maybe everything except purchases

---

8   Tasks like this are better induced by modeling or other, non-monetary incentives.

during a major trip at the beginning of each school year), and a high schooler could be responsible for pretty much everything but food and rent.

The idea here is that their allowance and their responsibility level both grow over time, but the proportion between the two of them should stay pretty consistent over time, Basically, you want their fixed allowance (part 2 and part 3 of the above chore chart) to be 80-90% of their total expenses in a normal week. This means that they still have to do some of their a la carte chores (part 4) in order to get absolutely everything they want. If they have a busy week, they can just do the minimum and still get by just fine, and if they have a high-expense week (like end-of-the-school-year parties, holiday gifts for friends, or some expensive toy they really want), they can make it up with extra chores (part 4).

One Important Caveat (That Can Throw the Entire System Out of Whack)

This is all well and good except for one thing that can render our entire system null and void.

Sometimes we are not the only source of money in our kids' lives. If you have relatives who like to spoil your kid with exorbitant holiday or birthday money, if you co-parent with someone out of your house (i.e. sharing time with a former spouse), or if your kid has any other ways of coming into money, it can ruin the system for one simple reason: it only works if your kid actually needs the money.

If your kids have more money than they know how to spend, they will have little to no incentive to do their mandatory chores, not to mention do extra.[9]

Except my little money hoarder. Children are weird. [Kristine]

If you have another party who is funneling cash to your kids, you might have to come up with some supplementary rules to ensure your children are still learning the right lessons about responsibility, saving, and the fact that they'll have to work hard to earn money as adults.

Possible fixes here include mandating that all extra cash has to go through you, insisting that your children save a certain percentage of the money they get as gifts in a long-term savings account, creating certain expenses that have to be paid with money they earn through you (e.g. they can't use gift money to buy things on your Amazon account, only money earned in the house), or just making them responsible for an even larger range of expenses (if the external money is consistent enough).

---

9   There will be the occasional child who just really loves to save. These super-human exceptions are my spirit animals, and you generally don't have to worry about teaching them financial skills. You *may* have to worry about them taking over the world, but that's really a different book...

A Note to the Thrifty Budgeters among Us

It may not have escaped your notice that even money your kids "earn" usually comes out of your budget.[10]

If your kids' tastes run to the extravagant and they have the time and energy to do all the chores in the world, it can actually run up a pretty large bill for you as the parent. It is at this point that you get the happy duty of teaching your child the joys of entrepreneurship.

> *I once overheard my son saying he'd like to be neighborhood gardener.* [Crystal]

Almost regardless of your child's age, there are ways to earn money outside of the house. Whether it's an elementary schooler running a weekend lemonade stand or a high schooler getting an after-school job, it is possible for your kid to earn money that doesn't come from you.

If your child's chores are starting to become a serious line item in your family budget, it is totally reasonable to put a cap on the amount of money they can earn inside the home. Make sure you explain why they have this extra regulation (because they should definitely understand that money doesn't grow on trees for you, either) and help them find external ways to earn money, but never feel guilty for making your kids operate within the financial realm of reality.

Cheat Sheet

Okay, let's break it down. This is the section where I give you actionable tips and practical strategies for how to implement everything we talked about throughout the chapter.

- Think out your system before your children ask for money. If you try and create a system when your kids already have dollar signs in their eyes instead of pupils, you're too late. (If this is you, it's still possible to get them on a system, but you're in for a bigger battle. Sorry.) When your children get to be around the age when they start understanding the concept of money (somewhere between ages 3 and 5), sit down and create a financial system for them that handles chores, allowance, extra spending cash, savings, giving, and all the other financial hurdles you're going to encounter. Taking 30 minutes of preplanning will save you roughly a decade-and-a-half of heartache.

- Some chores should be completely mandatory without any financial compensation. The type of chores that benefit your kid the most in the long term will be the ones they do to help out because they're a part of the family. Make sure you have a few jobs for your kids that are

---

10   Yeah, that part kinda sucks, doesn't it?

completely divorced from money, bribery, or other rewards. To get the full benefit, these chores should be things that help out the entire family (like cleaning common areas, caring for family pets, etc.), not self-serving chores (like doing their own laundry or cleaning their room).

• Don't pay your kids for anything if you want them to ever do it for free again. Paying your kids for something will kill their intrinsic motivation to do it. Paying them for reading? Congratulations, they may read like crazy when their wallet is empty, but they'll never pick up a book for fun again. Only pay for boring stuff like taking out the garbage, helping you stuff envelopes, and other tasks that are already pretty dull.

• Create a chore chart with an allowance that covers eighty to ninety percent of your kid's expenses. You want to make sure your kids have some needs that aren't covered by their basic allowance. This means they have to consistently engage the part of their brain that says "you need to figure out how to make more money". Whatever financial habits they build as kids will set the stage for their financial behavior as adults, so make sure they are developing the right habits.

• Help your kids with giving. Giving away their hard-earned money is not necessarily instinctive, but you want your kids to grow up thinking of people other than themselves. The average person donates roughly 5% of their income to charity ("Sam", n.d.) while some follow the Biblical rule of tithing 10% (Ramsey, n.d.). Whatever decision you make as a family, hold your kids to it. Don't let them draw into

This is no joke! Kids can sense weakness. **[Kristine]**

their "giving" money to fund their own purchases. That said, help make giving fun. If they like dogs, help them google animal shelters, and then let them walk their donation in in person so they can pet the dogs they're helping. Find a way to make giving personal, enjoyable, and fulfilling, and you'll help create kids who care about more than just their own purchasing power.

• Be consistent, and don't give in. The thing that can kill the lessons of a chore chart faster than anything is a parent who doesn't stick to the system. If your kid knows you're going to cave the first time they come to you with big puppy dog eyes and a sob story about how all their friends are going to the movies and they can't afford to go, then they won't have the necessary motivation to actually earn the money for that movie ticket by themselves. They don't have the urgency of a potential eviction or the fear of having to live off of ramen to motivate them, so it's your job as a parent to create as much motivation to earn as possible. This is what's going to drive them to start practicing the good financial habits you want them to learn.

- Actually, use a physical chore chart. It's important for kids to have a tangible way to record stuff. Whether you create one yourself or use the template I referenced earlier, have something that your kid can physically see, hold, and consult. It should roughly look something like this:

CHORE CHART

MY ALLOWANCE
Money I get no matter what.

TOTAL ALLOWANCE: $ _____

MY FAMILY DUTIES
Chores I do no matter what.

	MONDAY	TUESDAY	WEDNESDAY	THURSDAY	FRIDAY	SATURDAY	SUNDAY

MY WEEKLY JOBS
Completing all of these jobs earns my weekly salary.

	MONDAY	TUESDAY	WEDNESDAY	THURSDAY	FRIDAY	SATURDAY	SUNDAY

TOTAL SALARY: $ _____

MY OPTIONAL JOBS
Each of these jobs earns me a fixed amount of money per task.

	MONDAY	TUESDAY	WEDNESDAY	THURSDAY	FRIDAY	SATURDAY	SUNDAY

OPTIONAL EXTRA EARNINGS: $ _____

$ _____ + $ _____ + $ _____ = $ _____
ALLOWANCE   SALARY   OPTIONAL   WEEKLY TOTAL

Liz Bayardelle, Ph.D.

2

Get Straight A's

Intended Use: To make your child do well in school, which will hopefully lead them to a good college, successful career, and happy life of not living in a cardboard box

Possible Side Effects: Decreased intrinsic motivation, fear of failure, decreased learning, ignoring process goals, lack of big picture goals or ambitions

This one has come out of the mouth of almost every parent ever. I'm sure cave parents back in the stone ages groused to their kids about how little Ugg in the next cave over brought down a bigger bison than they did and why can't they practice hunting more.

Once your kid enters school, the obvious goal on everyone's mind is getting good grades. However, just like all of these sayings, the way you deliver the message can make all the difference.

Why We Say It

In 2011, Amy Chua came out with her extremely popular book *Battle Hymn of the Tiger Mother.* If for some reason you spent that year hiding under a rock (or in the North Korea style media blackout that accompanies the attempt to parent any child under four), it's basically a love letter to the strict discipline the author accredits to a traditional Chinese upbringing. It includes rules such as kids aren't allowed to play any instruments other than the piano or the violin, they aren't allowed to not play the piano or the violin, they can't have sleepovers, and—you guessed it—they can't get any grade other than an A.

Now, coming from a self-admitted, grade-grubbing, academic fetishist, type A personality (no pun intended), this didn't sound so bad. Piano is a pretty instrument, and I have an actual panic attack if I think about getting a B for too long[11] so Tiger Mom-ing sounded pretty okay to me.

And then I became a parent.

To say kids are complicated, hard-to-motivate creatures would be like saying the moon is a bit too far away to walk there for the afternoon.

There are many different types of kids. For example, my stepdaughter is insanely intelligent but cannot be convinced, as my southern relatives would say, "with two turkeys and a crowbar" to do something she doesn't want to do. My younger daughter is curious about learning absolutely everything but cannot hold still

> *Tough from a motivation perspective, awesome for resisting peer pressure.* [Crystal]

long enough to get to the fourth minute of an activity without doing five other things at the same time. Who knows what kind of crazy my son will end up being. (At

> *Squirrel!* [Crystal]

the time of writing, he's only a few months old so I'll give his persona some time to mature.)

What I'm saying is, regardless of what Amy Chua says, engineering a system in which kids get good grades is, in my humble opinion, way harder than just mandating that they get straight A's.

A Repetitive Disclaimer

You would be hard-pressed to find parents who haven't told their kids to try to get straight A's, or at least wished they would (while shame-eating failure donuts, sitting huddled in the back of the closet on report card day). It's not that unusual of a goal for a parent to have for their kids.

Now, before I go off on a verbal rampage, I would like to emphatically reiterate what I mentioned in the introduction: there's nothing wrong with the messages

---

11   I wish this wasn't a very true story.

behind any of these parent-isms. Every single statement mentioned in this book is said with the best intentions by amazing parents around the globe. Again, there is nothing wrong with wanting your child to get straight A's or do well in school. However, there is a translational issue between the parental desires that lead to the statement "get straight A's" and the way your child's brain actually processes and reacts to it.

So, why is it a bad idea to tell your kid to get straight A's?

Research Says (What They Hear)

There are several equally important reasons why it's not the best idea to have a straight-A report card as your child's only measure of success.

Reason #1: It Kills Intrinsic Motivation

The first reason why telling (ordering) your kid to get straight A's is that the act of simply telling your kids to get good grades will not make them want it.

If your first thought was "well, who cares if they want it?" you're not alone. This was my knee-jerk reaction as well. However, the answer is that you should care if they want it but not for the reason you think.

I truly don't care if my kids are short-term happy that I force them to study, practice piano, eat their vegetables, or any number of the behaviors we parents try to instill in our children to keep them healthy and turn them into adults who go to college and not to jail. I have zero percent concern for your broccoli-induced-tantrums, you tiny hedonist. Eat your darn veggies! Pick up a math book!

And for God's sake, go to sleep. [Crystal]

So, if you shouldn't care if your kid wants to get a straight-A report card out of concern for their preferences, *why* should you care if they want it? There's one seriously important reason: research shows that humans are more motivated to achieve a goal if they feel like they had a hand in choosing that goal (Ryan & Deci, 2017).

Basically, there are two types of motivation: intrinsic and extrinsic. The difference between the two makes all the difference in the world when it comes to how well motivation is sustained in the long term.

Extrinsic Motivation: The Carrot and the Stick

Extrinsic motivation forms the basis of most "typical" parenting approaches: getting your child to do something for someone else's reasons rather than their own. Take out the garbage, and I'll give you your allowance. Get good grades, or I'll take away your phone. When you hear extrinsic motivation, think carrot and stick.

Extrinsic motivation isn't just for kids, either. Do you know people who keep going to miserable jobs they hate because they need the paycheck? Blame extrinsic motivation. The desire isn't coming from them but rather from an outside promise of future benefits like the ability to pay rent without selling one's blood on the dark web.

The problem with extrinsic motivation is that it's not very effective. Studies have shown that people who are given extrinsic rewards for tasks actually perform worse on those tasks

> *Truth. In my house it's approximately zero percent effective. [Crystal]*

than those without external incentives (Eliot, Dweck, & Yeager, 2005). Not only does extrinsic motivation result in worse performance but also offering external rewards for a task actually decreases the internal desire to do that task from that point on.

You read that right. If you offer your kid an external reward for doing something, your kid will actually be less likely to repeat that behavior once the reward is removed (Deci, Koestner, & Ryan, 1999). As you learned in Chapter 1, this means that you can offer your kids $10 to clean their rooms, but the act of giving them an external reward will decrease the likelihood that they will ever clean their room of their own volition ever again.

I'll pause for a second while you rethink every parenting decision you've ever made.

I very nearly included a chapter called "do your reading" in this book for this very reason. (I decided against it because there was too much overlap with this chap-

> *Seriously? Like the toy chest at the dentist? *facepalm emoji* [Crystal]*

ter, but I still feel very strongly about the issue.) So, many parents force kids to do a certain amount of reading every day. Schools regularly send home mandatory reading logs. Heck, even my toddler's preschool has an optional reading log that, when completed, earns the kids a prize from a treasure chest they have in the classroom.

Sounds great, right? Because reading is important. Actually, this is dangerous because of what you just learned about extrinsic rewards decreasing motivation.

If you force a kid to read (or to get straight A's) with threats of negative ramifications if they don't or promises of rewards if they do, you are sending the subconscious message that they don't actually want to perform that behavior (i.e. reading, studying, etc.) because they need an external reward to get going. This means that the second you take away the carrot (or the stick), they will immediately desist in whatever behavior you were trying to create.

In the case of my preschooler, I actually hide her reading log and fill it out behind her back. She still gets the prize (because we read faithfully every day), but, instead of having it be a box she is forced to check to get an external reward for deigning to suffer through the activity, I actually have tried to present reading as a reward. Instead of presenting reading as work, I've gone full speed in the other direction. If she behaves badly, I threaten to take away her nightly reading time. It's literally the only threat she's never called me on. (Which, if you knew my toddler, you'd know is really saying something.)

Now, before you think I'm telling you to abandon your carefully arranged system of parenting based on threats and bribery, I'm not. It would be impossible to parent without using extrinsic motivation to some degree. These things do work—at least, in some contexts.

Research has shown that extrinsic motivation is fantastic for speeding up mundane, routine tasks that take no creativity and simply have to be done. Think assembly line workers or people stocking shelves at grocery stores. Statistics show these tasks are done more quickly and better with an external reward, so if your kid has to paint *Or just put on his dang shoes after being asked 7 times.* [Kristine] the house, deliver 100 flyers for a fundraiser, or bake a few dozen cupcakes for a charity bake sale, feel free to rely on extrinsic motivation to your heart's content.

However, for things that take focus, thought, or creativity, especially if they are things that you want your kids to develop a desire to do by themselves, you're going to need to foster some good old-fashioned intrinsic motivation.

Intrinsic Motivation

Intrinsic motivation is the desire to do something without any external reward whatsoever. When you think of intrinsic motivation, think of your kid the first week of any new activity, you know, the extracurricular honeymoon period in which all they want to do is practice dribbling in their new soccer cleats, do cartwheels in preparation for their next gymnastics class, or fool around on the piano. That glorious period of time between when you first sign them up for a new activity and when it starts to get old is the epitome of intrinsic motivation. They don't want to do it because you're forcing them but simply because they enjoy doing whatever it is they're doing and are authentically excited about it.

Having intrinsically motivated children is the holy grail of parenting. If you could create, bottle, and sell a way to induce intrinsic motivation, parents would flock to your door and within a year your bank balance would make Jeff Bezos and Bill Gates look like paupers.

Alas, it couldn't be that easy. Instead of a magic potion, we have to painstakingly lay the groundwork for intrinsic motivation within our children one behavior, one parental comment, and one sneaky parent maneuver (mom-neuver) at a time.

How exactly does one do it? How do you get your kids to be shiny-new-toy levels of excitement about things like reading, studying, and getting good grades? Glad you asked.

Creating Intrinsic Motivation

The psychological theory that talks about what makes humans do things is called Self-Determination Theory (SDT) (Deci & Ryan, 2012). Without going into much psycho-babble, I boil it down to four factors which I'll cover in a minute. If these four factors are present, your kid is going to be incredibly motivated to do something even without any tangible external reward. The less of these four factors, the more your kids will need external prodding to get stuff done. (A quick grammar note: I say *less* of these four factors not *fewer* because they are all sliding scales. It's not a present-or-not, yes-or-no type of thing, but rather how much of each one there is.)

Here are the four factors and what they mean to your kiddos:

Autonomy: This one refers to the degree to which your kid feels like they're in control of their own life. If you don't believe this has an effect, try an experiment. Let your kids pick a toy and time how long they play with it. Then, choose a toy for them and see how long it holds their attention. You experienced parents out there probably don't even have to actually do the experiment because we know exactly how it will play out. Basic SDT theory shows that adults are more motivated to do things they choose to do, and apparently kids aren't any different.

> *This is why I allow him to negotiate for a reward.* [Crystal]

Competence: This is the measurement for whether or not you feel like you're good at what you're doing. Everyone knows it's more fun to play a sport you've mastered than one in which you look like a bumbling idiot. It's more fulfilling to whip through a piano piece you know like the back of your hand than to attempt one for the first time and have it sound like a cat is being brutally murdered by a set of bagpipes. Self-determination theory research confirms the self-evident fact that it's way more motivating to do something when you feel like you're good at it.

Relatedness: This one speaks to the social nature of the task at hand. If an activity brings us closer to other humans we care about (whether it's friends, family, or those we're trying to impress like colleagues or teachers), it's more motivating than it would be as an isolated task. This serves double for teenagers who are in their "friends are all that matter in the world and parents should kindly stand a minimum of 15 feet away from me at all times thanks" phase, but it is true at all ages from toddlers to grownups. As social beings, we're more motivated to accomplish tasks that tie us in with those who matter to us.

Purpose: This one wasn't actually included in the original SDT but was later added to the model (Graham & Williams, 2009). Purpose describes how much an activity relates to a higher goal or calling. For example, kids might not be that motivated to do their biology homework just for the sake of it, but if they've gotten it into their head that they want to be a doctor someday, they'll buckle down with those ganglions like they're binge watching their favorite television show because their brain has classified their boring bio homework as a necessary step toward something they really want.

So, How Does This Relate to Straight A's Exactly?

These four factors related to the "don't tell your kid to get straight A's" thing because the act of instructing your kid to get straight A's violates each one of the four necessary components of creating intrinsic motivation:

- You're dictating their goal by telling them what they need to do, thereby depriving them of *autonomy*.

- The fact that you have to tell them means they probably aren't getting A's now so they probably feel less *competent* due to your comments.

- There is no social connection at all inherent in the concept of straight A's so *relatedness* isn't being generated.

- Finally, straight A's might be the means to future greatness (a lucrative job, choice of college, or a number of other amazing things in life that can only be attained with good grades), but the simple order to get good grades does nothing to convey the connection between A's and any kind of future *purpose*.

So, without intrinsic motivation, telling your kid to get straight A's is going to rely on extrinsic factors, like you bribing them to study or punishing them if they don't. As we discussed earlier in this chapter, not only is that almost always unsuccessful, but also it actually lowers the likelihood that they'll desire to get good grades once you stop bribing them to do so.

Or get A's to please me, while still learning nothing. [Crystal]

So, that's reason number one why you shouldn't tell your kids to get straight A's. Simply issuing an edict for a specific set of grades may cause them to begrudgingly try a little harder, but it will squash any internal desire for good grades from then onward.

Reason #2: It Creates a Fixed Mindset

The second reason why telling your child to get straight A's is a parental no-no is that it focuses their attention on the wrong goal.

Yes, technically having a piece of paper with a bunch of A's on it is going to make your child's pathway to Harvard much smoother than a paper with B's and C's on it, but it's not going to do them a darn bit of good once they get there. It'll matter even less out in the real world.

For you fellow grade-grubbers out there, I urge you to think of the class you remember the most from either high school or college. I can almost guarantee it wasn't the one in which you got an easy A; it's the ones in which you had to work your hiney off and still barely managed a passing grade.

Or the classes with crazy or charismatic teachers. [Kristine]

For me, the college class I remember best was an upper-level course on psycholinguistics. I somehow snuck in under the radar as an underclassman and was thrown into this class with a genius professor and only two other students, both of whom were seniors in the middle of writing their theses on various facets of linguistics I couldn't pronounce, not to mention understand. In the second week, we discussed the semantics of a single sentence ("It snowed on Baldy last night.") for two and a half hours.[12] I was in way over my head, but I was determined (read: stubborn as hell). I went to every office hour the professor offered. I met for extra study sessions with the two other students in the class. I seriously neglected my other classes. In the end, I snuck by with a B-, but I can tell you I remember more from that course than literally any other class I took in my four undergrad years.

This is reason number two why it's dangerous to tell kids they need to get straight A's: it focuses on the grade, not the learning. Once they get into college, no one will care about their transcript. In fact, they can get an A on an exam and not remember the material one bit the next day. That's not uncommon. Think back to a high school class in which you got an A. Do you remember anything? Me, neither.

Although we do want our kids to get good grades, it'll actually be much more beneficial to their long-term intelligence, learning, and success if we urge them to understand the material. Tell them to screw the test, but make them debate to you the merits of a democracy versus a republic. Help them make Spanish verb

I love this! Especially for a tactile learner! [Crystal]

---

12   Yes, it was that exact sentence. Yes, I'll probably remember it to my dying day. No, I do not want to talk about it.

charts until 3 a.m., make sure they know the difference between past perfect and past imperfect, and then take them out for ice cream even if they get a C.

No one is going to care about your kid's grades but you, the guidance counselor, and a handful of snooty admissions officers. It's your job as a parent to make sure your child is educated, intelligent, and comprehending, not just well-credentialed.

Reason #3: It Fosters the Wrong Behavior

On a related note, if you're looking to raise successful kids, setting the goal of getting straight A's fosters the entirely wrong set of behaviors.

The Joys of Cramming

We just talked about how it's entirely possible to ace a test and then wake up the next morning not remembering a thing that was on it. This means that studying to get A's doesn't necessarily mean learning, understanding, or retaining material. Fortunately, how much you remember from high school isn't tested as an adult. Approximately zero people would pass such a test.

However, people spend a decade or two of their life in the world of academia, and, as they say, old habits die hard. If you don't think how you approach school affects the attitude you bring with you into the real world, I challenge you not to have flashbacks to cramming for a high school test the next time you have to stay up late finishing a report. It's nearly impossible to do something for the first 20 years of your life and then stop cold turkey.

So, if you pressure your kids to get straight A's without differentiating between cramming and actually learning the material, then they will likely bring that last-minute, minimum effort to get the job done type of attitude to wherever they go next.

The Concept of Mindset

I would be remiss if I didn't take a moment to mention the book *Mindset* by Carol Dweck (2006). This is probably my all-time favorite book (other than *Added to my reading list. ETA for completion 2070.* [Kristine] the Harry Potter series) and one I heartily recommend to any and every human, parent or not. In fact, I think it should be given out at the hospital as required reading before you get to take your infant home.[13] Yes, it's that important to parenting.

The basic concept of mindset was born when Carol Dweck was doing psychological research with a group of children. The kids were doing puzzles of increasing difficulty and at some point inevitably reached one that was too hard for them to solve. She noticed that when they hit this point of failure, about half of the kids

---

13   This is probably why they won't let me be in charge of the hospital system. Rats.

got discouraged, lost interest in the task, or began choosing to do easier puzzles. This seems pretty logical. Failure sucks, and it makes sense that kids would want to avoid that icky feeling, right? Yes, for most of us failure is a bad, scary thing, but apparently no one told this to the other half of the kids.

When the second half of the kids encountered a puzzle that was too hard to solve, they got excited. Their interest in the task skyrocketed, and they asked for more hard puzzles, some even muttering things about how they love a good challenge under their breath. I don't know about you, but the first time I read this study I thought something along the lines of "who are these mutant children?" It turns out what Dweck discovered was the difference between children with something called a fixed mindset and those with a growth mindset.

The Joys of a Fixed Mindset

A fixed mindset grows from the belief that qualities like intelligence, athletic ability, or skill are, well, fixed. We have a certain amount of smarts, a certain amount of skill, and we can't really change it all that much.

This creates children who, when they reach a challenging puzzle, take it as an indication that their uncontrollable, fixed amount of intelligence has reached its end. They then have to deal with the ego blow that comes with this sign that they aren't smart enough, which led them to get discouraged, not want to do puzzles anymore (because who wants a reminder that you're not smart enough?), or do easier puzzles to get that warm fuzzy feeling of reassurance that they were smart enough to solve them. All this was happening on a subconscious level, but it was happening nonetheless.

This is all well and good for kids with puzzles, but it can be real trouble when you apply a fixed mindset to other areas of life. Running away from a hard puzzle is not that detrimental to a kid's life, but what about the kid who gets demotivated or angry at every missed soccer goal? What about the kid who wants to quit debate team at a first meet loss? What about the kid who works his or her butt off in a course, gets a B+ on a test (instead of the coveted A), and wants to drop the subject?

The first B after a genuine effort can be absolutely crushing. [Crystal]

Fixed mindsets are dangerous. Trust me, I grew up with one. It's not that uncommon, especially for kids who are told they are "smart" early on. If you are anywhere over the 50% mark in intelligence as a kid, grownups call you "smart" whenever you do a task well, quickly, or effortlessly on the first try. After enough repetitions, you internalize the connection between effortless task completion and being "smart." Then, the first time a task doesn't come quickly, intuitively, or on the first try, you have a horrible, sinking feeling: What if I'm not "smart" anymore?

This is why it's our job as parents to let our children fail early and often and to let them associate failure not with a lack of intelligence but rather with a lack of experience. Teach your kids that (almost) everyone fails on the first try, that success is what happens after a string of failures rather than from the absence of failure. Let them watch you struggle at things, push through, and then succeed.

One of the biggest dangers of fixed mindsets is that they lead people toward things that are easy. Yes, easy things are unlikely to lead to any challenge to your fragile ego, but they're also unlikely to make you learn, grow, or progress either.

Even scarier, a host of horrible behaviors accompany a fixed mindset. Fixed mindsets have been statistically linked to depression, lack of intrinsic motivation, cheating, defensiveness, and a bunch of other behaviors we want our kids to avoid like the darn plague (Conroy & Eliot, 2004).

Wanting your kids to get good grades isn't bad, but telling your kids to get an A could come with an unspoken "...and you're stupid if you don't". To ensure that challenges don't freak your kids out, that they don't tie external success too strongly to internal self-esteem, and to ward off the aforementioned negative behaviors that go with it, make sure your kids aren't looking at school (or any other endeavor) with too much of a fixed mindset.

Growth Mindset: The Healthy Alternative

The majestic, magical, unicorn kids who got excited when they encountered failure (in the form of hard puzzles) and wanted to double down on their effort when things got challenging possessed what Dweck termed *growth mindset*.

Now, before you deify these kids, I want to clarify that they were not more intelligent, more hard-working, or quantifiably better than their fixed mindset counterparts in any way. They didn't have higher IQs or better grades. What they did have, however, was freedom from the idea of intelligence as a fixed, unchangeable quantity. So, when they encountered a challenging puzzle, it wasn't a condemnation of their entire academic self-esteem or sense of intelligence, it was just a fun challenge they hadn't solved yet.

Without this link between failure and their sense of self, these kids were able to look at the challenging puzzles as more fun than the easy ones, the same way a kid will prefer the big kid slide over the one on the toddler section of the park.

This is the magic of a growth mindset. Humans naturally gravitate toward challenge, adventure, and exploration. When a fixed mindset ties the concept of failure to kids' self-esteem, it thwarts their drive to be challenged in favor of the easy win. They don't want to risk looking stupid (or unathletic or whatever quality they feel is being assessed) so they go for a task they know they're going to achieve, a class they know they'll pass, or a game they know they'll win.

Could Straight A's Actually Be...a Bad Thing?

Unfortunately, the problem with always going for the easy win is that you sacrifice all the learning that happens when you have to struggle. Kids who fight for straight B's in AP classes are usually smarter than those who got easy A's in their regular classes. Kids who practiced their butts off to make the B team in a prestigious sports club usually end up more skilled than the natural stars on the local rec team.

No, straight A's in and of themselves aren't a bad thing, but the act of *telling* your kids to get straight A's might be dangerous. If they know A's are the top goal, they're going to subconsciously (or consciously) gravitate toward classes that don't challenge them. They know there'll be hell to pay if they get a bad grade so they won't push themselves to get into that honors or AP class because it increases the risk that they won't get the perfect grade.

How to Give Your Kids a Growth Mindset

If you're a parent like me, you're now wondering (or furiously Googling) how you create a growth mindset in your kid.

First, if you notice fixed mindset traits, especially if you have an older child, it's not entirely your fault. The world as a whole usually focuses much more on outcomes (winning the game, getting the grade, getting into the good school, etc.) than it does on process. This creates a natural predisposition toward a fixed mindset.

There are some instances in which society has tried to correct this, such as the painful Little League teams where they don't keep score, but overall efforts are few, far between, poorly executed, and largely ineffective.

I, for one, am a firm believer in instilling a growth mindset in our kids, but I openly scoff at score-less games of soccer.

clapping hands emoji [Crystal]

Let's be honest, there is still such a thing as the real world. In the real world, there are quantifiable outcomes where people win or lose. Mindset notwithstanding, our kids need to be prepared for that world.

The best way to foster a growth mindset is to focus on process as much as you do on outcome, especially when it comes to setting goals. This brings us to our fourth reason why telling your kids to get straight A's is a bad idea.

Reason #4: Focusing on the Uncontrollable Leads to Heartbreak

I'm a huge fan of applying management and organizational psychology research to parenting,[14] and one of my favorites is a management book called *The 4 Disciplines*

You are my favorite nerd of all time. [Crystal]

---

14   Isn't everyone?

of Execution (McChesney, Covey, & Huling, 2016). This book talks about how a business can structure its goals and practices to massively improve performance. I'd highly recommend reading the entire book, but the part I want to mention here is Discipline 2, which encourages people to act on something called *lead measures*.

Lead Measures versus Lag Measures

Let's step into your kids' shoes for a second: your parents tell you to get straight A's, but as a kid you don't always feel like that's entirely within your power. Yes, sometimes a kid is just lazy and doesn't turn in work, but most of the time kids do genuinely try to get good grades. (None of them likes to see red ink scribbled all over a returned test or paper.) The problem is that they usually just don't understand *how* to get good grades.

This creates a huge, self-reinforcing problem. They want to get straight A's, but don't know how so they come up short. Then, their fixed mindset aims them away from things that could challenge them (and therefore make them smarter), so they learn less and less. With this decreased learning, it's even harder to get A's so they feel even dumber...and so on and so forth.

The problem here is that academic grades are what's called a *lag measure*. This is a measurement that happens after the behavior which determines it. In this case, the behavior that determines a child's grade (i.e. studying, reading, asking questions, doing extra homework prob-

Kind of supports the notion of the oh-so-hated pop quiz? [Crystal]

lems, etc.) happens before the grade is determined. By the time your kids know their grade, it's already too late to change any of the behaviors that would have affected the grade.

This is why it's important to set goals that prioritize lead measures. These are goals based on behaviors that come before (or lead) the eventual outcome. So, while a lag goal might be to "get straight A's," a corresponding lead goal might be to "study an extra 15 minutes each day on the hardest topic from that day's homework." Here the behavior that's being measured comes before the eventual outcome; kids are studying before they get graded on the test.

This way kids don't have the powerless feeling they might experience when you tell them to get straight A's. It might be a pain in the neck to study an extra 15 minutes a day, but it's totally within their power and capability to do so.

The Art of Creating Lead Goals

Even if you completely make the shift from lag to lead in terms of what you ask of your child, the world still operates on lag goals. No one cares how much your kids study (especially as they get older) because all that matters is how they did on the test. No one looks at how hard your kids worked in high school, only the name of the college to which they got accepted.

It's hard fostering lead goals in a lag-goal world, so here's where your job as a parent begins.

Your first job is to learn how to create lead behaviors that directly affect the eventual lag measure. This means you have to figure out what "right now" behaviors are actually going to bring about success on the ultimate final metric. Will studying more lead to an A on the test, or will extra homework help more? Is it better to make flashcards or just reread the textbook?

Basically, lead goals only matter if they ultimately bring about success on the metric society actually cares about: grades. You have to find the things you can set as lead goals that will bring them the successes the world cares about (i.e. grades). Unfortunately, that's the easy part.

Your second job is to teach your kids how to figure out *by themselves* which lead goals will bring about their ultimate success on any given challenge. They won't always have you sitting at your computer printing out extra math worksheets. In college, they'll need to be able to take a class, analyze the material, and figure out which study methods work for that specific class. In the big, scary, real world, they'll need to analyze the cues they get from their boss and figure out which behaviors are going to bring them success in the workplace.

The only real way this happens is by trial and error. This is expected but does mean that the A might not come immediately. This is why you need to rely on some metrics other than "you had better get straight A's, kid" while the two of you figure out how to do it.

Reason #5: It Prioritizes the Wrong Long-Term Achievements

So, reasons #1 through #4 were very hands-on, but this one is a little more abstract. It is, however, no less important.

The final issue with telling your kids to get straight A's is that, unless they're academic fetishists, the idea of getting straight A's isn't actually all that exciting for a kid. Even if they would technically like to have good grades, it's nowhere near as exciting as getting a new toy or playing with friends. (Think back to how we talked about

Except for those of us where it is. Just saying. [Crystal]

autonomy, relatedness, competence, and purpose creating intrinsic motivation.)

The reason for this is that people are way more motivated to accomplish something if it's an emotionally charged goal (Bagozzi, 1997). While A's might be all well and good, they probably aren't emotionally connected to many things your kid cares about.

If you can relate good grades to something larger that your kid wants, on the other hand, they'll be way more motivated to study. Has your kid always wanted to get into a certain college? (Maybe where a sibling went?) or wanted to be a doctor since playing with a toy stethoscope as a toddler? Saying "get straight A's" won't harness these emotions but saying "you need to get good grades if you want to be a doctor" will be much more effective and motivating.[15]

This isn't always easy because some kids don't have solidified career ambitions when they're in elementary school. Some don't even have them when they're in high school. In these cases, you'll have to get creative, but I guarantee you there is something your kid does care about (even if it's really hard to determine). If you can pinpoint the areas of actual passion and relate things to what they really care about, you're bound to have more luck than with a dry, impersonal goal that is more of a priority for you (or for the sake of societal norms) than it is for your kid.

Cheat Sheet

Okay, maybe I've convinced you that telling the kiddos to get straight A's isn't the best idea, but what should you say instead?

First, let me really throw you for a loop by saying you actually *can* say "get straight A's" to your kid without plunging them into a lifetime of criminal activity and mismatched socks. The really important part is how you present it, how they understand it, and (most important) the behaviors that come after you tell your kid to get straight A's.

That said, here's the dummy's guide to how to steer your child toward academic accomplishment in a more healthy, productive, and ultimately successful way:

- Regularly connect academic achievement to big-picture success in real life. Mention in conversation that you hired someone at work who went to Harvard. Talk about how you used your middle-school algebra figuring something out the other day. Tell them stories about fun college classes. Tell them the academic pathways that lead to the profession they can't stop talking about (even rock stars need to know math for accounting and good writing skills for business proposals and pitches to record companies). Make their grades their ticket to what they want, not something they have to suffer through before they get to pursue their dreams.

- Give them as much autonomy as possible. Make it their idea as much as you can (within reason and without sacrificing outcome). This applies not only to their reasons for getting good grades but even more so to how they get there. Ask them how they *Especially for parents of kiddos who learn differently.* [Crystal] think they study most effectively. Let them choose the location, time of day, etc. The more they feel autonomy over the process, the more motivated they'll be.

- Don't destroy their self-esteem. This sounds pretty obvious, but inherent in any parental request for good grades is the subtle (sometimes not so subtle) insinuation that they're dumb as a stump for getting bad ones in the first place. Remember, feelings of competence are necessary for motivation so try to make your kids feel smart as often as you can.

- Emphasize learning over grades. If your kid studies really hard and masters the material but still chokes on the exam, try taking him out for celebratory ice cream, anyway. If your kid happens to ace a test but doesn't really study or you know she didn't actually know the material, don't make a big deal of the A. The more you emphasize learning (remember the benefits of a growth mindset), the more ambitious, interested, and passionate your kids will be.

- Find and enforce process goals. Make sure you remember the difference between lead goals and lag goals. Find the behaviors that will lead your kids to good grades and then enforce the behaviors, not the grades. For example, time them for 20 minutes of focused time rereading their textbook each day, and then compare the results to when they made flashcards and quizzed themselves 20 minutes a day. Analyze what behaviors create the results you want, and, more important, teach your kids to analyze their own options and make their own study plans.

3

Don't Be a Quitter

Intended Use: To keep your kid from bouncing from activity to activity until you are broke, frazzled, and frustrated and they are slightly better than mediocre in many different things but actually excellent at exactly nothing

Possible Side Effects: Preventing critical skill development and exploration, delaying the development of prioritization, boundary setting, and decision-making skills

Your kids want to try out ice skating. They're jittery with excitement for their first class. They come home glowing and talk of little else for the next week. They ask for new ice skates for Christmas, they start saving up their allowance for new gloves to wear during their lessons, and you start Googling how to be the parent of an Olympic ice skater. As the weeks turn to months, the excitement slowly starts to wear off. After a few weeks, they no longer look forward to classes with as manic a level of excitement, and after a few months, they start outright complaining or asking not to go.

If this is your first rodeo (i.e. the first sport or extracurricular your kid has tried), it's probably no big deal. You let them stop and pick another activity because you don't want to drag them to something they no longer enjoy.

So, they decide try soccer. You see the same manic excitement and the same letter to Santa requesting new cleats, but this time you're cautious. However, there's nothing that wears down your resolve like the excitement of your progeny. After a few weeks, like Charlie Brown with the football, you are somehow convinced you have the next Mia Hamm on your hands. Unfortunately, this lasts for about as long as the ice skating phase did, and pretty soon you're dragging your kid to practice by the hair.

Lather, rinse, repeat.

It's heartbreaking to see a kid start something with the potential for insanely awesomeness but then give up before having a chance to get good at it. This is something we all see as parents.

Why We Say It

Anyone who has parented a child over the age at which they start doing extracurriculars has noticed that kids seem to bounce from activity to activity like a pinball in a box of meth. They hang in there just long enough for you to cave and buy them all the gear, supplies, or paraphernalia needed to master whatever that month's activity is and then magically lose interest a few weeks later.

After a few years of this, your garage is full of baseball gloves, art supplies, hockey sticks, tutus, and goodness knows what other artifacts, each dating back to a 2-4-month period when your child wanted to be the next virtuoso at you-name-it.

Before we go into why this happens, I want to reassure you that it's completely normal. You are not a bad parent. You did not raise a hedonistic sociopath with ADHD. (Well, you might have, but you'd need to confirm it with a heck of a lot more evidence than just sport hopping.)

That's just how kids are.

If gyms in February are any indicator, adults too! [Crystal]

Research Says (What They Hear)

There are indeed instances in which kids need to be told to tough it out and finish what they started. You aren't supposed to let your kid bounce from thing to thing with zero discipline or direction.

In high school, my family got to be close with the family of one of my volleyball teammates. and I kid you not, their family motto was "suck it up, princess."[16] I don't mean as a joke; I mean the kind of family motto you find needlepointed onto throw

---

16   Just a quick disclaimer, this was not said in a derogatory way in terms of gender. It was said equally to my female friend, her 6'2" brother, and her father. The only population that should feel remotely insulted is helpless Disney princesses.

pillows. This statement was brought out any time someone began whining because they didn't get what they wanted. We're not going to the movie you wanted? Suck it up, princess. You have to study for your final instead of going to that party? Suck it up, princess.

I mention this because, while a host of lessons can be learned by granting your children the autonomy to start and stop their activities at will, they will need to tough it out through some situations when it's easier to just quit.

Sick of soccer in the middle of a season? Sorry, but you made a commitment to your team. You don't have to play next season, but for now...suck it up, princess.

Have stage fright about that piano recital even though you've been practicing all month? You'll have to perform in public (speeches, business meetings, presentations, etc.) your whole life. It's a learning experience. Suck it up, princess.

Only you as a parent will be able to judge whether response to a circumstance reflects "quitting" (in a bad way) or simply choosing not to do something anymore. Situations are very rarely clear-cut, but the section below should help you decipher which times you should let your kids decide their own fates and which merit a swift and firmly stated "suck it up, princess."

So, to get at what kids really hear, let's go over some reasons kids do bounce from thing to thing and, more important, why it's important for them to do so.

Reason #1: Exploring, Not Quitting

It's important for kids to try new things. (Duh.)

There is an astounding number of different activities your kid could excel in, from drama to volleyball, swimming to debate, pottery, Spanish classes, photography, robotics. Today's era of parenting superkids has led to a truly frightening array of activities your child could do. Sign language for toddlers? Classes all over the place? Coding for elementary schoolers? Take your pick. Martian cooking for former fetuses? Probably exists somewhere. I wouldn't be surprised.

This variety is good and bad. It's good because kids need to try a bunch of things to find "the one" thing that they actually want to focus on for the long term. Very few kids find the activity they'll still be loving when they're adults on their first day of preschool. Many don't find it until much later. Julia Child learned to cook in her late 30's. Stan Lee drew his first superhero at age 43. Laura Ingalls Wilder wrote *Little House on the Prairie* in her 60's.

Yes, some people know what they want to do with their life before they learn to read, but a far larger portion of successful people took their time in finding their true passion.

The reason kids bounce from thing to thing is they need to experience a huge variety of activities to pinpoint exactly what they like to do. The odds of you as a parent sticking them in an activity when they're still in diapers and having it be the exact perfect fit for them long-term are astronomically low.

It's more likely that you'll put them in ballet, only to realize that they really spend most of the time hanging from the bar rather than dancing. You then switch them to gymnastics (so they can hang off bars properly), where they discover that they're way faster at running down the vault runway than all the other kids. You put them in track, but they can't get excited about running in a straight line for hours on end. Then, one day they go to their friend's house and play around with a soccer ball, so you decide to give that a go. They like it for a few years but eventually lose interest. Then, one day they randomly pick up a lacrosse stick, and the stars align. There's a burst of golden light (think Ollivander's when Harry finally picks out the correct wand), and angelic song fills Dick's Sporting Goods. They find a sport that merges their super speed with the strategy they learned in soccer, and they never look back.

Just like you aren't still working at your high school summer job, it takes kids a while to figure out what they like, what they're good at, and what they can be passionate about in the long term.

If we penalize kids for "quitting" or, worse, label them as a "quitter" every time they switch activities, they run the risk of staying in something just for continuity's sake and missing out on finding their true passion.

Reason #2: Skill Development

The next reason kids can, will, and should bounce from activity to activity like a raccoon who got into a garbage can of Halloween candy is that they need to build a wide variety of skills.

First, and this may be a hard pill for some of you to swallow, very few of our kids are going to grow up to be professional athletes or Olympians.

pauses while you throw a pair of children's hockey skates across the room in a fit of parental rage

Remember that kid we talked about before? The one who bounced from ballet to gymnastics to track to soccer only to end up playing lacrosse? Yeah, he's going to end up being a CPA or a contract lawyer, lacrosse or no lacrosse.[17]

Kids don't usually play sports (or do drama or take art classes) because that's going to be their ultimate profession. I, for example, played volleyball for 15 years. Other than the fact that I get irrationally, golden-retriever-puppy-with-a-new-ball levels of happy when volleyball comes on TV, the fact that I spent four hours a day for a majority of my formative years having balls hit at my face does not have any *direct* impact on my adult life.

Except for having the trained instinct to duck toddler-hurled objects. [Crystal]

---

17   Yeah, you thought it was a girl because I mentioned ballet? Ha! Gotcha. #genderstereotypes #boyscandoballettoo

However, it does have an immeasurable amount of *indirect* impact on my adult life. Having to keep running during the fifth round of wind sprints when all I wanted to do was lie down (and possibly puke) taught me a kind of persistence I use when it's 11 p.m. and I still have work to do even though I'd give anything for a few hours of sleep before I have to get up and feed the baby. Working toward a common goal with less-than-pleasant teammates gave me important skills for my first experience with less-than-pleasant coworkers (and many other bunches of unpleasant humans I've encountered since). Creating a long-term plan to improve my jump serve by a certain date (e.g. club tryouts, state finals, etc.) gave me hands-on experience with goal setting, planning, and self-improvement strategies that I use every day for, well, pretty much everything I do.

Just because our kids aren't going to be on the world cup soccer team doesn't mean that they won't use the teamwork, discipline, and drive they learn playing on their local AYSO team. This means that, since odds are they aren't going to be on the Olympic podium, the purpose of all these extracurriculars is to help them learn as many valuable skills as we can cram into their tiny heads. This critical skill set doesn't necessarily include throwing the perfect curve ball, but it does include other things they'll learn through their extracurriculars. An emphasis on acquisition of life skills over subject-specific skills is why it's not necessarily a bad thing if your kid hops from thing to thing, especially in the younger years.

Reason #3: Learning to Balance Their Time

One of the biggest lessons that extracurriculars teach our kids is how to balance their time.

During the school day, kids are ushered from one mandatory activity to another. The teacher tells them where to go, what to do, and how long they have for each activity, ensuring they always have enough time to finish each one.

If you found yourself salivating at that description, congratulations, you're officially a parent. We have a million places to be at any given moment (and we are the ones who have to schedule it all). We have more tasks on our to do list than any five humans could ever accomplish in a 24-hour period (and we have to pick which ones are most important and face the fire if we choose wrong). And we will never actually have time to complete anything before our tiny gremlins start demanding we play with them, help them with homework, or explain why Fifi, the household bulldog, can't fly.

This is why extracurriculars are important. This is the first taste your kids will get of choosing their own activities in a scenario where you can't do all the things. They have to pick which activities to do, which to neglect, and come to terms with the principle that time spent on one activity isn't being devoted to other ventures. They'll learn that they can spend a little time on a lot of things and become mediocre to good at all of them, but that if they focus a lot of time on one thing they can become really good at it.

Yes, it's important to teach kids to stick with things, but it's also important for them to learn to weigh the value of different ventures and pick the one that's most valuable in the long run, even if it means stopping something else. It also means that your kids have to learn not to commit to more things than they can do well, a skill we all wish we had a little more of from time to time.

Reason #4: Good Quitting as an Adult

This last reason brings up one last, very important skill: learning to say no to things.

Whether it's a promising opportunity to take on more at work, a fun thing you desperately want to do, accomplishing more on your to do list to the detriment of a good night's sleep, or simply prioritizing various claims on your time, saying no is one of the hardest things an adult has to do.

What is this magic you speak of? [Crystal]

The art of gracefully declining an opportunity or politely saying you don't have time to do something is incredibly challenging.

It also happens to be an insanely important skill for any adult who doesn't want to live an unimaginably frazzled, and overbooked existence. Learning how not to book yourself for more than you can do (and do well), how to recognize when you're in over your head, and how to figure out which things to cut out when you have to scale down are essential life skills that need to be taught in childhood.

Is this done? [Kristine]

What To Say Instead

There are some occasions where instead of telling your kids not to be a quitter, you should help guide them through the process of properly deciding to change life course. They'll have to do this numerous times in their lives, from changing jobs to ending relationships, so they need to know how to do it well.

When to Let Your Kid Quit

Here are some of the situational characteristics that usually indicate it's okay for your child to stop something they're doing:

- It's something they just began doing and found they don't like.
- It's an activity they have done for a long time (years, not months) and their interest has been slowly declining.
- They have other activities they are doing for the long term.

- Their primary motivation for continuing the activity would be not displeasing you.

- They tried an activity because it's your favorite thing, but they don't enjoy it.

- The desire to quit comes from being overscheduled or too busy.

- They have an alternative activity they want to substitute for the one they're quitting.

- It's an "optional" activity rather than something school-related.

- They can clearly enunciate why they want to stop.

Basically, let's say your kid just wanted to try out a passing interest in violin lessons, and, surprise, it turns out didn't like them. It doesn't matter if you played violin all through your childhood and have an undying passion for it. Your kids shouldn't be forced to play their way to a university scholarship. Make them stick it out through their first recital (providing training in grit and delayed gratification), but then let them stop playing and try something else.

Similarly, if your kids have been doing gymnastics since they did Mommy and me as a toddler, they used to love it but they have been steadily losing interest over the course of six months, and they come to you asking to quit gymnastics so they can try out for the school swimming team, help them do it properly. Have them write thank you notes to the coaches who have been a part of their lives since before they could talk, make sure they quit at a time that doesn't let their team down, and then get them a new bag for their swim gear as a celebration of their new direction.

When Not to Let Your Kid Quit

On the other hand, there are many circumstances that merit a "suck it up, princess." Kids do need to be forced to stick with things sometimes or they will turn into flighty, undependable, messes as grownups.

Here are the indicators that this is more of a "suck it up, princess" type of moment:

- The primary motivation for quitting is that the activity just started to get challenging.

- They want to quit immediately following a big loss or other let-down.

- They have developed a pattern of serial quitting, where they do activities for a few weeks and then get tired of them.

- They don't have any interest in doing any other activities as a replacement.

- They have plenty of time in their schedule and are not time stressed due to the activity.

- They want to quit due to social reasons rather than for a reason related to the activity itself.

- They made a commitment to other people, such as a team, group, partner, or someone else who will be negatively impacted by their quitting.

- They don't have any activities they have pursued long-term (years, not months).

- They recently asked for (and got) expensive supplies or equipment for the activity.[18]

- They can't explain in words why they want to quit.

Overall, no one but you can know when your kid needs to tough it out and when they should be allowed to choose not to do an activity. I only encourage you to think it through rationally. Try to disentangle your personal feelings about the activity itself and look at what your kid is gaining from the experience. (Remember, very few kids grow up to be professional whatevers. It's all about the learning.) Weigh the benefit they get from the activity and their motivations for stopping.

When all else fails, listen to your kid. If they can explain their reasoning and it sounds like they've thought it through without any major logical gaps, congratulate them on a choice well-made and help them transition to whatever comes next.

Cheat Sheet

- Teach kids the difference between "quitting" and "choosing not to do something anymore". Usually quitting is based on a hedonistic desire to take the easy way out of something that just got hard or unpleasant. On the other hand, your kids have to be able to have a way to stop an activity which they genuinely tried but no longer enjoy.

- Sometimes, kids need to suck it up, princess. There will be times when your kid isn't allowed to quit or isn't allowed to quit just yet. Make sure they get good at following through on their commitments, taking no for an answer when it's necessary and knowing why they have to master the art of finishing what you start.

---

18   This one is especially important if they have a track record of starting something, demanding all the "stuff" for it, then quitting shortly after. You aren't made of money. and it is doing yourself *and* your kids a great disservice to let them think you are.

- Teach kids how to make decisions about how to spend their time. There's no way your kids will have the time, energy, or finances to pursue every activity that strikes their fancy. Teach them how to prioritize, analyze what matters and will benefit them in the long term, and how to organize their schedule to get the most benefit out of their activities.

- Teach kids how to say no. Saying no to a potential activity is hard. Many (if not most) adults still have a hard time with this one. Start showing your kids that they can't do literally everything, and help them learn to politely decline opportunities they don't have the bandwidth to do well.

raises hand slowly [Crystal]

4

Don't Talk Back (to Your Elders)

Intended Use: To keep your kids from mouthing off to you and whatever other significant authority figures they have in their lives

Possible Side Effects: Decreased situational awareness, lack of critical thinking skills, and a difficulty to stand up to peer pressure and authority figures alike

The latter bit of this one sounds a little old-timey, but the overall message comes across loud and clear in many statements that you still hear all the time even though we no longer travel by horse and buggy.

Why We Say It

Like knocking your entire just-prepared dinner to the ground. [Kristine]

The basic premise of "don't talk back" stems from one simple truth: kids are jerks. Actually, to be more accurate, toddlers are tiny terrorists, small children are jerks, and teenagers are, well, best described using words I'm not comfortable putting on paper. It makes total sense that parents of any era would have spent a large portion of their time and energy telling their kids not to talk back. If left unchecked, talking back would probably be all kids do.

However, despite the insanely necessary message of not talking back, there are some understated messages conveyed in this one seemingly unavoidable sentence that can give your kid a lot of un-learning to do later on in life.

Research Says (What They Hear)

First of all, before you chuck your book across the room, let me bring your blood pressure down a few notches.

I am not saying you should let your kids run around being mouthy little twerps. On behalf of society at large, I think I can solidly affirm that you most certainly should *not* do that. In fact, as a parent, you should probably do everything in your power to ensure your kids master the fine art of holding their tongue. Please, for the sakes of their future spouses, coworkers, and all of the rest of us who will have to deal with them throughout life, don't let your kids grow up thinking that they can or should say whatever thoughts pop into their twisted little minds.

Mean comments can and should be kept on the inside. Pointless or hurtful gossip should be consistently contained by the majestic (though unfortunately metaphorical) mouth filter. There are many things that your kids should be taught not to say, and it is your unfortunate yet solemn duty to indoctrinate the little monsters to the wonderful world of biting your tongue.

I am most certainly not advocating you let a single rude, hurtful, profane, or otherwise unacceptable word exit your child's mouth uncorrected.

Childhood versus Real Life

So, if you still have to install the mouth filter on your tiny monsters, what's so bad about telling them not to talk back? Isn't it especially important that they not start mouthing off to their teachers, relatives, and other significant adults in their lives? This sounds like a trap.

The problem isn't with talking back, but more with the message this conveys about how your kids should relate to authority figures. Statements like this create a paradigm which works perfectly throughout childhood and even into their teenage years (to some extent) but can be unhelpful, maladaptive, or downright dangerous once your kids enter the "real world."

Let's start with childhood.

It's probably a good thing that your small child learn that she needs to heed what the teacher says. One of the first lessons kids learn as they begin to develop "socialized behavior" is to listen to the adult in the room without questioning, do what the adult says, and remain as quiet as possible while doing it. This basic principle is important as it enables kids to learn and play in large groups without accidentally reenacting *Lord of the Flies*, preschool style.

As kids get older, they learn more about the superpowers of their authority figures. Parents teach them everything from house rules to life lessons, dictate a large part of their daily existence, and, at least until your child becomes a teenager, your unquestioned omniscience is incredibly reassuring to your child. My 4-year-old often asks, "How do you know that?" and she doesn't even blink when I answer "because I know everything."[19]

I am so using that one the next time. [Crystal]

Kids need to think that the adults in their life are all-knowing, all-powerful, all-encompassing authority figures because it's the only thing keeping their tiny worlds from feeling chaotic and scary. If our infant knew about the "can you believe they're actually letting us walk out of here with a baby" conversation my husband and I had before we left the hospital maternity ward, he probably wouldn't feel very safe or secure. It's this unadulterated faith in grownups that allows us to comfort, teach, and nurture our kids. So, for the period of childhood, it's not maladaptive at all. It's necessary.

And then they grow up.

A child with complete trust in and obedience to adults is thought of as the perfect child. College students who never question what they are told is thought of as naive (at best). Members of the workforce who never question what they're told are total morons.

This is the crux of the issue when it comes to not just shouting, "Don't talk back!" at our kids every time they start talking like catty little brats. Learning how to think for yourself is one of the most important transitions from childhood to adulthood. Instead of focusing on the short-term goal of having them not be rude little hellions (which is an incredibly tempting goal when you're being publicly screamed at in the middle of the towel aisle in Target), we need to devote more thought and energy toward the broader goal of teaching your kids how to properly relate to other humans, including the fact that it's not okay to scream at you in a public place.

It's All about Subtext

This doesn't seem like it's that big of a distinction in the early years. Saying "don't talk back" is basically the same as saying "it's not okay to talk to me like that," right? Wrong. The difference lies in the underlying message that's getting conveyed to your munchkins.

---

19   Man, will I be heartbroken when this is no longer the case!

Telling your kids "it's not okay to talk to me like that" conveys a basic message that their current behavior is inappropriate in that situation. Even though this is a magnificent understatement, it is nonetheless true. However, when you say "don't talk back," the underlying message is that there's a hierarchical relationship between the two of you and that they need to stop mouthing off, disagreeing with you, or just generally getting on your nerves because you are higher up on the food chain than they are.

This is not necessarily untrue in childhood, but, as we'll discuss next section, they're going to need to know how to disagree with people who are higher up on the food chain later on in life. They'll have bosses who are occasionally wrong and need to be respectfully questioned. They'll have significant others they desperately don't want to lose, but with whom they still need to be able to have disagreements.

The Art of Disagreement

> *My son has perfected the art of disagreeing with me.* [Crystal]

Your child will not (and should not) agree with everyone they meet in life. This begins with their idiotic preschool arguments about whose turn it is on the slide, progresses to middle school fights over who copied whose fashion choices, through the terrifying teenage onset of romantic relationships (and all the disagreements they cause), and into adulthood where workplace conflict has to be handled in a professional, logical manner.

There is actually a large branch of organizational psychology that suggests that conflict within a workplace, when handled properly, can actually be a productive force within an organization (DeDreu, 2007). No, we don't want our kids to be disrespectful little jerks, but we also don't want our kids to grow up to be boring, conflict-avoiding yes men (or yes women).

So, how do we find the middle ground here?

What To Say Instead

Believe it or not, when you tell a kid not to talk back, you're actually trying to teach your kid critical thinking skills.

(Don't worry, if you accidentally snorted a mouthful of partially ingested coffee at the idea that your goal could be anything other than making your kid sound a little less like Veruka Salt on steroids, I promise I'm going to back this up with an explanation. Wipe up your coffee and keep reading.)

Let's put it in terms of what thought process you're trying to trigger in your child. I'll go through the two different scenarios in terms of a multistep process that goes on in your kid's brain. First, here's the sequence for the statement, "don't talk back to your elders."

Sequence #1 (Don't Talk Back to Your Elders)

Step 1: Hark, the majestic maternal goddess speaks!

Step 2: Silence, peasants!

Step 3: Listens intently and follows directions to the letter.

Ahhh, parenting expectations versus reality. [Kristine]

Although in the moment it might feel like getting your kid to follow this thought sequence would basically be winning parenting in a glorious way, that's not actually the thought process you're trying to install in your kid's brain. First of all, it's not very realistic. Second, that's not the way you want your kid to respond to authority figures or other people they care about.

If you go back and reread the sequence, only instead of imagining your kid is listening to you, you picture them listening to their first (and entirely unacceptable) boyfriend or girlfriend, the joy you initially felt will rapidly transform to either horror or poorly-controlled rage. As tempting as it is when they're small and you're the only major figure in their lives, you don't want to train your child that absolute obedience is the way to gain someone's affection or approval.

What you really want is train your kid to think properly and rationally. Compare the following sequence to the sequence #1:

Sequence #2 (It's Not Okay to Speak to Me That Way)

Step 1: Evaluates the situation, including what they want to gain and how they disagree.

Step 2: Takes into account the position, trustworthiness, and perspective of the speaker.

Step 3: Carefully weighs potential courses of action (and their consequences).

Step 4: Responds strategically and respectfully.

The first thing I want to point out is that, in that scenario where your kid is mouthing off to you, both sequences are likely to yield very acceptable answers. Yes, sometimes we might desire absolute and unquestioning acquiescence to our every whim, but if our kid responds with a respect-

And a well-negotiated challenge actually creates better compliance. [Crystal] ful, well-thought-out challenge or question to our initial request, who among us would be anything but super proud?

So, given the fact that you're okay with the outcome of either sequence, why teach your kid to think along the lines of sequence two? It comes down to what you're teaching them. Sequence one teaches your kid compliance whereas sequence two teaches critical thinking.

Let's walk through it step by step.

Sequence #1 Example (Learning Compliance)

Say you're in that Target aisle and your kid is screaming at you to buy the latest X, Y, or Z and you said no. (Should be easy to picture.) Under Sequence #1 your kid simply hears you say no, shuts up, and swallows any disappointment because you're bigger, stronger, and hold all the power.

This might work when your kids are small, but later on they will be more likely to follow this same pathway when a significant other pushes them to do something they're uncomfortable with, when a boss gives them an instruction they have a moral problem with, or when a friend asks them to do something that they know they shouldn't be doing. It sucks, but you're not always going to be the only important figure in their lives.

Sequence #2 Example (Learning Critical Thinking)

If you break out Sequence #2, using that hellish Target trip, you can achieve the same (actually better) results and teach them some life skills to boot:

Step 1: You help your kid evaluate the situation: a public place where shouting is unacceptable. Then, the kid rationally defines the problem: a desired toy that you don't want to buy.

Step 2: The kid acknowledges that you are the mom. This means you are entitled to a basic level of respect as a human, a member of the family, and the person who takes care of literally all of his or her needs. Ideally, acknowledgement is made that you hold the credit card and get to make the final say on purchasing.

Step 3: The kid takes a second to consider options: agree not to get the toy (and maybe gain some maternal good will for later), respectfully talk you into it, work out a repayment plan, etc. It doesn't matter so much what options are suggested so much as the kid realizes that there is more than one option and that he or she is in control.

Step 4: The kid attempts to facilitate the chosen course of action in a respectful tone of voice.

Disclaimer: High Effort Equals High Reward

This one is definitely going to be more work for you. You basically have to walk kids through that entire mental process every time they have a verbal explosion until they get it through their thick little skulls. It's going to be a huge pain in the neck.

Alexa, add Ibuprofen to my shopping list. [Crystal]

However, if you apply Sequence #2 to a different scenario, it's going to hold up in the real, adult world as well. Sequence #2 means that your kids will be able to be amicable and respectful while staying firm and not sacrificing their own values when that boyfriend or girlfriend tries to push them too far, that friend tries to make them do something unethical, or their boss is clearly wrong about something but they don't want to get fired.

Teaching critical thinking is essential to your child's success, both in adolescence (Williams & Worth, 2001) and in adult life (Zifkovic, 2016).

When You Should Actually Talk Back

Before we get to your Cliff notes section, there is one very important point I want to note. Sometimes, your kid is going to need to talk back.

If my kids are in a situation where they feel their safety, comfort, or moral principles are being threatened, you better bet I want them to talk back as quickly as possible. I want them to be loud, rude, abrasive, and completely comfortable in doing so.

They do need to know that situations in which this nuclear option is necessary or desirable are incredibly rare, and they should be fully aware of the consequences of their actions if they choose to take this route. However, if my kids get into a situation where someone is trying to get them to compromise on something that's essential to their wellbeing, I want them to feel completely at ease telling whoever it is exactly where they can stick it.

Even though the idea of having a completely complicit child is something you may secretly fantasize about while dealing with a screaming, tantruming toddler, or a shouting, petulant teenager, it's not actually something any of us want. We want kids with backbone, sound moral compasses, and the ability to think for themselves. Don't crush the desire to talk back out of your kids completely, just hone it down a little bit with critical thought.

The Whole "Respect Your Elders" Thing

I touched on this briefly above, but I wanted to reiterate this very important fact: just because someone is older than you are, that does not make them smarter, righter, or more knowledgeable than you are.

While kids need to follow the general rule that they should listen to adults, it's a good idea to give them another reason to do so other than just age. Taking the extreme minority case first, a stranger asking your child to get in their white van would technically be an "elder," but one you definitely want your child to ignore and disregard.[20] A coach, family friend, or other "elder" could be a potential pedophile asking your child to keep their crimes a secret. This would be another elder you desperately want your child not to listen to or respect.

While these minority cases are incredibly unlikely to happen to your child, they do prove the point that you don't want your child to listen indiscriminately to all adults. This is where you teach them critical thinking.

They don't obey someone because they are an adult; they obey them because they are an adult who has proven to be trustworthy and to have their best interest at heart, because they are a teacher and your kid knows that everyone has to follow the teacher's instructions or the classroom would descend into utter chaos, or some other logical, explainable reason.

Except when it comes to pants wearing. [Crystal]

The days of "because I said so" are gone. You want your kid to know why it's important to obey so they can also pinpoint instances in which they shouldn't.

Cheat Sheet

- Teach how to express emotions properly. Often, kids act out or mouth off because they don't have the emotional skills to express their feelings in a more constructive way. When your kids are being disrespectful, take it as a challenge, and help them translate whatever big, uncomfortable, scary emotion they are feeling into a respectful, logical statement that can be said at a normal volume. This will take the patience of Job and all the tongue biting in your arsenal, but it's one of the most important life skills you can teach.

- Teach when it is and is not an okay time to ask questions. There are times when your kid needs to listen immediately whether they like it or not. This isn't times like "when Mom is mad" but rather issues of immediate safety or other critically important issues. If your kids run into the street, they can't pause to ask why you want them back on the sidewalk; they need to react immediately. If they're being loud during a funeral, they need to know that you get to tell them to be quiet without explaining why. Explain that there will occasionally be

---

20   And probably report to the proper authorities.

instances when they have to listen without question, but that they can always ask questions later, after the immediate danger has passed. Make sure they know these situations will be few and far between, but that when they come your kid has to react immediately and ask questions later. If it helps, you can set up a code word that you can use only for these "no questions" situations, but make sure you really do only use it in an emergency.

- Probe for deeper thought. Your kid won't know how to diagnose a situation correctly the first time. Or the first hundred. You have to model the way to ask the right questions about a situation to lead them Socratically to the right answer. When they start mouthing off, try to rationally lead them through the thought process they should be having so they arrive at the better behavioral alternative. For a little kid throwing a tantrum, this will sound something like, "Okay, so what are you feeling? How can you say that in a way that will make me want to listen to you? Do you think this is the right time to discuss that?" and so on. For an older kid or a teen, it might be "Is so-and-so a person whose opinion matters to you? Do you have to obey for a good reason, or do you just want them to like you? What is your opinion on the topic? How can you respectfully disagree without damaging the relationship?" or something along those lines. Regardless of the answers generated, teaching your kids to think through a situation is essential to raising critical thinkers.

- Teach perspectives. Kids start out only thinking about things from their own perspective. It's your job as a parent to teach them to see situations from multiple angles. Instead of their reptilian hindbrain shouting "I WANT THE TOY" at the top of its metaphorical lungs, they should know that they want a toy, you want to make them happy but don't want to spoil them, brother didn't get a toy and would be upset if things weren't fair, Dad is worried about spending too much money, and so on. The earlier your kid starts realizing he or she isn't the only person in the universe, the better it will be for everyone involved.

- Teach to whom they should and should not listen. Babies come out of the womb trusting everyone. As parents, we try to do our best not to break this trust. However, we also have to teach them that not everyone they meet is going to be as well-meaning as we are. In real life, kids can't know right away whom they shouldn't trust and need to have a process in place for figuring out if a person is trustworthy.[21] Make sure kids know that not everyone is an equally credible source, which adults (or people) should be listened to and which should be politely disregarded, and how to tell the difference.

- Teach respectful disagreement skills. The most important thing here is to teach your kids how to have an amicable disagreement. While you might want your small children to just obey you and be quiet, don't waste those important opportunities to teach your kids that they can have a difference of opinion with someone whose opinions they care about without damaging the relationship.

---

21 I have a tremendous problem with kids' movies on this front. In almost every kids' movie, the villain is immediately identifiable because they are ugly, old, fat, dressed in all black, campy as all hell (cough cough Ursula cough), or obviously "evil" in some other way. And if that doesn't give them away, you can always see if there's spooky music playing in the background every time they enter the room. I talk about this in depth in a later chapter, but I wanted to mention it here as well because (as you can probably tell) it is a subject about which I feel very strongly. Parents, please teach your kid that bad guys look just like good guys and that you can only tell which is which by looking at people's actions over time. Thank you for coming to my TED talk!

5

Waste Not, Want Not

Intended Use: To keep your kids from taking more than they need, wasting things others could use, and other general hoarding behaviors

Possible Side Effects: Even more manic hoarding, binge eating, and unnecessary amounts of guilt

We've all heard this one. This statement got whipped out early and often in our childhoods: any time we didn't finish our dinner, got an outfit that we didn't wear, or bought something we didn't actually need. It was right up there in frequency with "eat your food because there are starving children in India" on the list of maternal guilt trips.

Why We Say It

The overall message is good. As a species, we have gotten to the point where we consume way too much material junk, a large portion of which we don't even need. According to the NRDC, Americans currently waste away about 40% of our food, throwing it away completely untouched (Gunders, 2017). The fact that parents are trying to get kids to be more conscious about not wasting things is extremely necessary, especially given the nature of children.

I Tell a Tale of Tiny Hoarders

If you've ever spent any time around kids, you know they have an irritatingly natural proclivity toward what can only be described as hoarding.

Basically, they are a cross between Hobbits and House Elves. [Crystal]

Kids seem to run on the philosophy that more is always better. If left unsupervised around candy, the average toddler will literally eat until sick. If you offer kids something they don't really care about (or have no idea what it even is), most will take it simply because having things is better than not having things. Just attempt to clean a kid's room and you will be knee deep in the evidence that the urge to acquire things (even if you don't really need, want, or even understand them) is baked into a child's genome.

As irritating as it may be, this urge makes evolutionary sense. On a large scale, human children are relatively small, helpless, and fragile. A baby horse walks minutes after birth. Wolf pups are eating meat when they're only three weeks old. Yet humans are still mostly dependent on us for survival, protection, and assistance with their day-to-day tasks for at least the first decade of their lives. Given the relative fragility of human children, it makes sense that the ones who hoarded resources (especially food) would be more likely to survive than those without this impulse. Just look at how small a baby's stomach is or how often your toddler gets hungry, and you'll see why having a backup stash of things would have come in handy back in caveman times when food was scarce.

However, what may have been evolutionarily beneficial back when we were hunter gatherers is now inconvenient when you open your child's backpack and find a collection of rocks they found on the way home, enough stick figure drawings to make the Louvre look minimalist, and approximately 147 pencils, a majority of which you most certainly did not buy for them. We've had to fight the battle where each year our kids want new school supplies every year, yet we

You have a random rock and stick collection too? [Crystal]

have begun to amass a truly alarming quantity of unopened pencil packs, notecards still in their shrink wrap, and other completely unused leftovers from prior years. Whatever follows in this chapter, I want you to know that I know as well as any parent the very real dangers of childhood hoarding and wasteful behaviors.

Research Says (What They Hear)

When you say "waste not, want not", the message you are trying to send to kids is that they shouldn't take more than they need and then waste a portion that they don't want. To you, this statement infers all kinds of amazing things like conservation, selflessness, consideration of others, and other incredibly important messages. These are noble, accurate, and incredibly necessary things for parents to teach kids.

Unfortunately, your kids are hearing exactly none of these things.

When you say "waste not, want not," your kid isn't hearing, "you should consider how hungry you are before ordering so the restaurant doesn't have to throw away perfectly good food that could be going toward the growing population of food-insecure children in our community." They're actually hearing "shove that extra piece of pizza in your mouth whether you want it or not or you're going to get into trouble."

Now, I'll go over the specific perils of the "clean your plate" philosophy in Chapter 13, but right now let's focus on the fact that there's a gorilla-sized disconnect between what you thought you were saying and what your impressionable little sprog actually heard. This is never a good sign.

What To Say Instead

The broad idea behind this statement is that your kid isn't the only person on the planet. This might come as a surprise to some kids, especially if they're in that super fun-to-parent spotlight effect (lovich, Medvec, & Savitsky, 2000) phase of teenagerdom, but it is sadly the case.

As parents, the sooner our children learn that they exist as members of a global community, the sooner they stop acting like entitled little asshats (hopefully).

This chapter is unique because instead of saying that the parental saying in question unintentionally sends a bad message, this one really just doesn't go anywhere near far enough in terms of covering why it's important not to waste. It's much quicker to just rely on a quick saying that will (ideally) get your kid to stop bugging you for new toys when they already have 15 barely-played-with ones at home, but it won't convey the really essential lessons that will turn your kid into a truly amazing human later on in life.

Leveraging Life Lessons: Conservation, Unselfishness, and Service

Like most parenting issues, these big questions are best handled early, often, and before an actual situation arises. I'm sorry to inform you that if you find yourself screaming "waste not, want not" at a teenager who is demanding yet another trip to the mall (in spite of a closet full of barely-worn clothes), you've already lost the battle.

As you go about your day-to-day lives, start looking for opportunities to show your kids the need in the world around them, the ways people act wastefully, and the ways you can reduce waste. Teach them about the people who could be in need in their own community. When you go out to eat, ask them what they think happens to all the food people don't eat. Help poke holes in their egocentric little worldviews so they begin to notice that there is usually a finite supply of things and that when they take more than they need, it could deprive someone else.

This is an issue with band-aids, tape, and dental floss. [Crystal]

The Majestic Power of Modeling

That's why I hide in my room to scream obscenities. [Kristine]

One last, yet incredibly powerful, parenting strategy that should be mentioned here is that kids respond way better, faster, and more strongly when behaviors are demonstrated than when the child is just being lectured over and over again.

If you tell your child not to over-serve themselves, they may or may not listen. However, they might start to catch on if you talk to them as you're making up your own plate and show them that you're only taking a small scoop of ice cream because you're not that hungry and you don't want to face the decision of whether to eat more than your stomach can comfortably handle or to put perfectly good ice cream down the drain later. Maybe if you walk by something in Staples and mention how it's really pretty but that you already have a similar one you barely use at home, they'll start to think along those lines themselves. Parenting is far less what we tell our children and far more what they see us do when we think they're not watching.

Modeling is an intensely powerful psychological phenomenon (Grusec, 1992). If parents can take advantage of the power of modeling, it makes our job easier, our teaching more effective, and our lessons more likely to stick in our children's minds. Model the ideals of conservation, frugality, and unselfishness, and your kids are sure to take notice.

Cheat Sheet

- Only take what you need. The short term solution to this issue is to teach kids how to appropriately gauge their own needs and to help them practice doing so accurately. Try asking them how hungry they are on a 1 to 3 scale, where 1 is just a snack, 2 is a small meal, and 3 is absolutely starving. Ask them how many clothes they think they should own based on how much is possible to wear in the average week and how often you do laundry. The more you talk to your kids about gauging their various needs, the sooner and better they'll be able to make these judgements for themselves.

- Don't say yes all the time. If you are one of the many parents who express their love with gifts, toys, and goodies, you may want to consider some alternatives at this point. Gifts are a perfectly acceptable way to make your kids feel special every once in a while, but if you're whipping out the wallet every time they ask for something, you're creating a system for them in which money, objects, and their access to them is unlimited. The unfortunate consequence of this is that they will start placing less and less value on things, which will in turn make them more and more comfortable wasting them. Not only is it bad for them (and for your wallet), it's also setting them up for a pretty high bar or a pretty large disappointment later in life when they're the ones paying the bills.

- Become more comfortable with scarcity. Kids get inherently nervous when they think there won't be enough of something. We talked about the evolutionary basis for this, but in the modern age it's very unlikely that your kid needs to hoard all the pizza slices at the dinner table to avoid going hungry. Teach your kids to start with a small amount and get more later if they need it. The more comfortable your kid is with the idea of reasonable scarcity, the easier it will be to train the hoarder out of them.

- Make your kids aware of need in their surroundings. Point out need when you see it. Are there kids at their school who qualify for the school-bought lunches? Do you drive by homeless people on the way to the grocery store? Do they have friends in worse financial situations than your family? These are often things people try to ignore out of discomfort or politeness, but make sure your kids both see these things and understand what they mean. Have the awkward conversation. Take them to volunteer. The more aware your kid is of those in worse situations than they are, the less likely they will be to waste and the better human beings they will be in general.

- Teach alternatives to wasting. I'm from Colorado so this approach was deemed the "use every part of the buffalo" approach in my childhood (BBC, n.d.). Teach your kids to think creatively about what to do with the things they aren't going to use. Plan a leftover night into your weekly menu. Let them help you take their old clothes to a charity. Use old school supplies or broken toys for art projects. The more creative you can get with this, the more your kids will start thinking along these lines as well.

6

Be Nice to Your Friends

Intended Use: To keep your child from antagonizing literally everyone they see, talk to, go to school with, or otherwise encounter in life

Possible Side Effects: Decreased quality of actual friendships, a higher tolerance of abusive relationships, or increased likelihood of your kid putting themselves in dangerous situations

As anyone who has ever talked to a toddler can tell you, toddlers can be brutal. Like, soul-crushingly, life-ruiningly frank. There's a lot of truth to the Internet meme that says "if a woman calls you ugly, she's jealous; if a man calls you ugly, she's flirting, but if a kid calls you ugly...you're ugly."

Kids have absolutely no sense of social niceties. They also occasionally spaz out with small bursts of poorly-controlled demonic meanness of unknown origin. (No, it's not just your kids. It's all of them.)

Why We Say It

The fact that parents across the globe tell their kids to be nice to their friends is entirely unsurprising. We're terrified our little monsters will alienate their peers and doom themselves to a life of social isolation and misery (sticking us with the therapy bills).

However well-meaning this parental plea for our kids to exercise their still-developing mouth filters may be, it does still have some unintended consequences.

Research Says (What They Hear)

Despite the fact that you do in fact want to ensure that your kids aren't rude, little, demon spawn, you telling them to be nice to their friends before they go to school, as a warning when they start to act up at the park, and as they go into a brand new situation can send two pretty harmful messages:

- Everyone is your friend.
- You have to be nice to your friends no matter what they do.

So, let's look at these two important constructs involved in the parental edict "be nice to your friends:" the concept of nice and the concept of friends.

Niceness, Respect, and Childhood Turrets

First, let's take a second to acknowledge the ambiguity in the concept of being "nice".

Say your coworker comes up to you and asks if you like his shoes. You look downward only to be immediately blinded by an abhorrent medley of colors so bright it may qualify as a traffic hazard. Is it "nice" to tell him that you like his shoes?[22] I mean, lying to people is supposed to be not nice, right? But so is hurting people's feelings. If you were to honestly inform your obviously color-blind coworker as to the human rights violation situated around his metatarsals, would it qualify as "nice" or "not nice"?

Regardless of the correct answer to the great shoe debate, it illustrates the important point that being "nice" isn't always as clear-cut an instruction as it sounds. Not only does the definition of "nice" contain a lot of grey area, it also differs dramatically from person to person.

In this shoe example, if the coworker is a relatively new acquaintance the "nicest" thing to do is probably respond with a polite dodge or mild white lie to save feelings while contemplating the quickest way out of the situation. However, if it's someone you have worked with for years and have developed a strong and resilient

---

22   Bet you thought this was a woman, right? Check your gender norms, pal. Men can have ugly shoes, too.

friendship, the "nicest" thing to do might be to tell the brutal truth, possibly in a humorous way that reaffirms the strength of your friendship.[23]

So, if there is a fair amount of grey area in the concept of niceness for adults, you can see that it would be even more difficult for children who are still learning the different protocols for basic social situations.

Each parent might handle this nebulosity in a different way, but I personally think that it's much more helpful to kids to use more concrete concepts in your parental requests.

Politeness

This is the first concept I would introduce to most children, as it is usually considered to be a universal constant. I wouldn't want my children to be affectionate to everyone, nor would I necessarily like them to even be friendly to everyone. (In fact, we are trying very hard to train our 4-year-old not to be so friendly to everyone. Seriously, the people behind us in line at Starbucks really don't need to know about our dog's potty training accidents. Tone it down, Smalls.) However, there are very few exceptions to the rule that your children should be polite to most of their fellow humans. Unless someone is actively abducting, assaulting, or otherwise violating your children's basic rights, they should probably treat all people with basic politeness. This includes things like not screaming at people, keeping their hands (and feet and teeth) to themselves, not saying objectively mean things, saying "please" and "thank you" when appropriate, and maintaining a basic sense of decorum and social consciousness as they bumble their way through early life.

Parenthood: the cure for the Common Introvert. [Crystal]

While this might not be easy to train your kids to do, it isn't very hard to teach them when it needs to be done. You can safely try to train your kids to default to a baseline of polite behavior without much grey area. Basically, act like a human, not a monkey, and you should be good.

Respect

The next level up from politeness is respect. While politeness is something to which all humans are entitled, respect should (at least in my opinion) be earned.

It's not hard to earn respect. The litmus test I use for my kiddos is that, if someone treats you with a basic level of respect, you treat them the same way. However, if someone is rude, hurtful, or otherwise disrespectful, my kiddos know they have my full blessing to choose not to interact with that person. They still have to be polite as they nope their way out of the situation (because almost everyone is entitled to a baseline of politeness), but they don't have to subject themselves to someone who doesn't treat them the way they should be treated.

---

23   I don't know, but I'll let you know when my retinas heal.

This distinction comes in handy when dealing with some of the more old-timey perspectives. By this, I mean things like telling a boy to "turn the other cheek" when someone bullies him or telling a girl that a boy is allowed to treat her a certain way just because he asks her out or buys her dinner. The difference between politeness (to which almost everyone is entitled) and respect (which must be reciprocally earned) helps your kid deal with things that used to be societal norms but have since proven to be counterproductive (or downright creepy).

To sum up, I'd say politeness is the global rule that your child should be as courteous as is situationally possible, whereas respect is a deferential way of treating people that is earned only by reciprocity.

Friendliness

This one really kicks in around the ages of two to three. Your kiddo is so excited to show off burgeoning social skills that all the sudden the kiddo is best friends with every kid around, the checkout clerk at the grocery store, that lampshade over there, the stray cat sitting on your car, and your newly-planted nectarine tree (literally...my kiddo named it "Friendly," and they talk every morning)[24].

It's a fantastic sign that your kid is willing and capable of creating social bonds with so many different people (and the occasional inanimate object, I guess). It means their verbal skills are blossoming and that you have done a great job as a parent in making them feel safe and secure. Give yourself a high-five.

Friendliness Downside #1: Issues of Safety and Childhood Stranger-Friends (aka Dear Toddler Please Stop Telling Strangers Our Address)

When reading the last paragraph, it may not have escaped your notice that, while we want our kids to feel safe and secure, the world they live in is not an entirely safe and secure place. Far from it.

While there are very few long-term downsides to your toddler having pretend conversations with a plant, there are very real consequences to a child being too friendly with the wrong type of people. Telling strangers where you live or when you're going on vacation could increase your risks of a robbery or home invasion. We all know the horror story of a child trusting a stranger that says he'll show them a new puppy if they only come into his house or get into his car.

While we want our kids to feel safe, happy, exuberant, and friendly, they also have to know that they have to marry these qualities with an appropriate serving size of caution and common sense as well. Teach your kids that while they should be polite to (almost) everyone and demonstrate respect with (almost all) those who respect them in return, friendliness shouldn't be exercised indiscriminately. Things

---

24   True story: my teenager saw an ant crawling up my toddler's arm and attempted to blow it off for her. My toddler shielded the ant and screamed "Nooooo! He's my best friend!" My teenager didn't stop laughing for days.

like physical contact, sharing of personal details, and feeling comfortable being alone with a person should be reserved for those who are truly your proven and long-term friends. This means people you know well, people who have proven to be trustworthy, and (for littler kids) people who have been approved as "trustworthy" by parents.

Friendliness Downside #2: Emotional Dangers (aka A Tale of Cookies and Neediness)

As your kids grow up and start school, they stop having indiscriminate conversations with lampshades (hopefully) and enter a much more complex social realm. While it might seem like, with the increasing social competence of an elementary, middle, or even high schooler, the dangers of friendliness have passed, this is actually not the case.

And now I would like to tell a tale of the worst (and most incorrect) social lesson I ever learned—and how it took me the subsequent decade to unlearn it.

If you couldn't tell from my biting sarcasm and fervent insistence on a strict adherence to grammatical intricacies, I didn't have the easiest time making friends as a child. The briefest explanation of my particular social problem is this: A child who is raised by wolves never learns how to eat with a salad fork. As the only child of incredibly intelligent parents (with whom I was and still am insanely close), I never really learned how to relate properly to other kids. I was much better at talking to adults and actually became friends with many of my teachers.[25] As you could probably guess, this did absolutely nothing to endear me to my peers.

In high school, after a solid decade of wondering just why I didn't fit in, I discovered two of the girls in my English class who were in the technical theater group (i.e. the people who do the lighting and paint the scenery for the drama club) had "hell week" that week and would be staying at school until 9:00 or 10:00 at night every day until the show opened. That night, I showed up at the theater room at 8:00 p.m. with a giant tray of warm, freshly baked cookies. High schoolers are ravenous monsters so it will surprise exactly no one that this gesture was very appreciated (and the cookies rapidly consumed). Like the good little Skinnerian rat I am, I then showed up with cookies the next four nights and, by the time the show opened, I had successfully baked my way into my first friend group.

Now, if any of you were thinking ahead about what conclusions my developing mind might have been drawing from this experience, you probably just experienced the literary equivalent of the background music that is played in a horror movie as the side character walks down a rickety staircase into a poorly-lit basement.

---

25   When I say I was friends with my teachers, I'm not kidding around. My sixth grade English teacher let me knit in her class. My second grade teacher is still considered to be a close friend of our family. My high school geometry teacher and I still email at least once a month, and she sends my kids stuffed animals from fun places when she and her husband go on vacation.

What adolescent Liz took from Cookiegate was the fact that if you just performed acts of service for other people you can make them like you. Extraordinary! There's no conceivable downside to this whatsoever! Nothing can go wrong now!

Yup, everything went wrong. I then spent the next decade of my life trying to bake, buy, lend, toil, and work my way into friendships with people who had no real desire for a reciprocal friendship (or later a mutual romantic relationship) but were plenty content to consume the goods and services I was only too happily offering. What I "learned" in one week of adolescent cookie baking took me a half-decade to realize was a horrible idea and another goodness knows how many years to stop doing. Even now, as a (mostly) secure, happily married, mother of three, I still have to tamp down the urge to try to buy people's affection (usually with food).

If only for my sake, please tell your kids early and often that they should not bestow their friendliness on anyone who does not willingly and freely offer it in return.

Kids are often told to be friendly or to be nice to their friends in order to ensure they have a social network. I've definitely been tempted to tell my violence-prone daughter that no one will want to be friends with her if she didn't stop accidentally hug-tackling them. However tempt-

Except her male counterpart; my son lives for hug-tackles. [Crystal]

ing this line of thinking may be, try to ensure your kid gets the message that friendships are born from mutual compatibility and interest. No one has to "earn" friends' attention via friendliness or anything else.

Affection

The final tier on the relational hierarchy is the demonstration of affection. This can mean physical demonstrations of affection (e.g. hugs, holding hands, pats, kisses, etc.) or it could just be verbal expressions of affection.

Kids should be taught two primary things about affection:

1. Affection is reserved for those close to you who have earned your trust.

2. You never have to show anyone affection if you don't want to.

Let's go over these one by one.

#1: The Relationship Hierarchy

With our affection-prone toddler, I've started using the categorization of strangers, acquaintances, friends, and family. Strangers are people you've never met, acquaintances are people whose names you know, friends are those you have known for a while and who have earned your trust over time, and family is those members

> *This made me laugh out loud – sooooo true!* [Kristine]

of your tribe (whether related by blood or mutual weirdness) whom you trust implicitly in all circumstances.

Kids should know that these categories exist, how to place people in the proper category, and that their behavior toward people will vary depending on what category that person is in. They should know that most of their classmates are acquaintances and not friends, and they should know that this is completely okay. Not everyone has to be their friends, nor should they be.

By saying "be nice to your friends" insinuates that everyone they meet that day should qualify as a friend. Not only is this rarely ever going to be the case, it also gives your kids false expectations of the hellishly brutal social atmosphere that awaits them just inside the doors of their school. Your kids should be polite to everyone, but they shouldn't be expected to show friendliness to the kid who tries to bully them in the lunch line, the jerk who makes a snide comment about them in homeroom, or any of the other horrible inhabitants of your child's social landscape.

Exhibiting politeness to (almost) everyone will keep your child from becoming the bully, but there is no reason we can demand or should desire that our kids be friendly to everyone.

#2: Affection Is Voluntary

The entire next chapter is devoted to this concept, so I won't go into it in too much detail, but ensure your kids know that they are never obligated to show affection. Affection is the top level of the polite-respect-

> *... and self-initiated.* [Crystal]

ful-friendly-affectionate behavioral hierarchy and should only be demonstrated when it is 100% authentic and heartfelt.

Forced affection is not only disingenuous for the recipient but it is also a violation to ask someone to demonstrate a feeling they might not have. This top level of the hierarchy is completely voluntary, and your kid should know that no one can or should ever demand this if they aren't feeling it.

What To Say Instead

As discussed above, your kids should know the difference between friends and acquaintances. This is important because, as they go through life, a vast majority of the people they meet will never proceed past "acquaintance" to "friend". This is okay, normal, and good.

There is an overwhelming notion especially around small children that they should be friends with everyone. "Let's all be friends!" is the rallying cry of preschoolers everywhere, yet it couldn't be farther from the case. Any adult can tell you that a true friend is someone whose loyalty, common interests, and compatibility have been tested extensively and have held true over time. Having a real friend, who likes you for exactly who you are, isn't afraid to tell you when you do something stupid or get an ugly haircut, and appreciates your bizarre sense of humor is both incredibly rare and immeasurably valuable. Most adults have at maximum a handful of people they consider to be true friends, and *My sentiments exactly!* [Crystal] these cherished weirdos hold an irreplaceable role in our lives.

Given this incredibly high bar for the concept of friendship, it seems kind of silly to expect our kids to form this kind of bond with everyone in their classes. Heck, it's a pretty high ask for them to be expected to find even one or two true friends by the time they finish high school. It's totally fine for you to expect your child to be pleasant, polite, and respectful, but insinuating that they can or should be friends with everyone they encounter is just setting them (and you) up for disappointment.

Schemas for Dummies (and Your Child)

There is too much information in the world for your child (or you, or any human) to absorb and consider each fact individually. Our brains simply don't have the processing power. We would be stuck so indefinitely trying to process all the information available to us that no decisions would ever get made, no actions taken. So, to help us make sense of this incredibly information-rich world, we use mental shortcuts to help us reach mostly accurate conclusions in much quicker ways.

Schemas, one such mental shortcut, are basically preconceived groupings of interconnected information (Torney-Purta, 1991). For example, if something has four feet, fur, and barks, it's probably a dog. We don't have to assess its exact coloring, behavior, ear size, or other features to know that it's probably a dog. We then activate our schema for "dog" and know exactly how we should treat that barking, four-footed, furry thing. Even if we've never met that particular dog before, our schema for the concept of "dog" helps us know how to act. Our brain can create a fairly accurate guess at how we should act while taking a very small amount of time processing information.

The reason schemas are relevant in this section on friendliness is that your child has schemas for everything. Information your child gathers about the people they meet, situations they experience, and types of encounters all get sorted based on their preexisting schemas.

Typical childhood schemas are for things like "friend," "trusted adult," or "bad guy". Usually, this works to your children's advantage. They can assess a new situation fairly quickly and, using their schemas to guide their behavior, know exactly how they should act at any given moment. Is this new kid a "friend"? Then I should probably be nice, share my toys, and wave goodbye to them before we leave the park.

However, where your kids can get into hot water is when they select the wrong schema for a given situation. For example, what if your child meets an adult at the park and instead of triggering the "stranger" schema, your kid activates the "trusted adult" set of behaviors? You can see how a mistake like this could have serious ramifications. After all, schemas are mental shortcuts, and shortcuts mean that you're sacrificing some accuracy for a higher degree of expedience. There is a chance that, in not processing all the information, your child will come to the wrong conclusion and activate the wrong schema.

Quick Rant: This is another reason why Disney movies (and other made-for-children media) make me incredibly mad with their depictions of villains. By constantly presenting the villain as a fat, ugly, or old character who wears all black and is accompanied by creepy music, they are giving your kid the misperception that real life "bad guys" will always come with these schematic clues. In real life, bad guys look just like good guys and cannot be easily identified on sight. In real life, you have to devote some real time to getting to know someone before you can tell if they are a "bad guy" or a "good guy." Stop making our kids think that they're safe around someone as long as they don't cackle, twirl their mustache, or carry a sinister-looking walking stick. End of rant.

So, what do schemas have to do with not telling your children to be nice to their friends? Simple. They need to know that, when they meet a stranger, they have to activate the "stranger" schema even if the person looks nice, acts nice, or offers to give them free candy or show them a cute puppy. They should know that they should use the "acquaintance" schema for kids in their class until they earn the status of "friend." Later on, when they begin dating, they need to know that it's okay to downgrade someone from "potential romantic partner" or even "steady boyfriend" to "molesty jackass" the second they push them to do something they're not comfortable doing.

Kids need to know what schematic categorizations exist for the people they'll encounter, what behaviors they should show in each situation, and that people have to earn their titles as "friend" or "trusted adult" with long-term behavioral consistency.

The End Goal

The end goal is a child who is confident in many different types of situations, from meeting new peers or adults to correctly interacting with people they've known for years. Children should have appropriate schemas of what behavior is appropriate for what type of person, and they should be able to tell who falls in what category. Most important, they should know that, while politeness should be a universal constant, they are not obligated to show respect to those who do not demonstrate it in return. They should know that friendliness is reserved for people who have earned the title of friend, and they should feel confident in the fact that affection is a 100% voluntary way of expressing their feelings toward a trusted member of their tribe, blood-related or not.[26]

If your kid can internalize these categorizations and their corresponding sets of behavior, they will have a much easier, safer, more successful, and less painful time navigating their social surroundings.

Cheat Sheet

- Teach the behavioral hierarchy of politeness, respect, friendliness, and affection. Your kid should know that their behavior has to be different based on whom they're interacting with at any given time. Teach that politeness should be a constant, but that respect, friendliness, and affection should be reciprocated and earned via good behavior (on the other party's part) over time. They should also know that if someone does not treat them with the appropriate level of respect (or friendliness or affection) it is acceptable and expected to downgrade them without hesitation or guilt.

- Teach the difference between strangers, acquaintances, friends, and family. Strangers are people you've never met before, acquaintances are people whose names you know, and friends are people you have known for a long period of time and have earned your trust. Once kids get this categorization system, you can start helping them put their actions into perspective. They will know what is acceptable behavior for a friend versus an acquaintance and how to tell the difference.

- Teach reciprocity and a willingness to walk away from one-sided relationships. Your kid does not need to go above and beyond for people that would not do the same for them. There are 7.8 billion people in the world. Your child cannot be friends with all of them, so your children get to select which ones make the cut. If your child has someone who is not as invested as he or she is in the friendship, teach your kid that it is not mean and is actually perfectly acceptable to walk away. Politeness must still be shown (because almost all humans deserve politeness), but no one should ever feel the need to stay in a one-sided relationship.

---

26   Some may have a different opinion on this, but it is my fervent belief that not all blood relatives are family and not all family is blood related. Family (or one's tribe, if you like that term better) is the word for people you trust implicitly to put your best interests over their own. This is the highest schematic ranking a person can achieve (in my book), and the title should not be used loosely.

7

Give Your Aunt a Hug

Intended Use: To get your kid to show respect and affection for close members of your social circle or important adults in their lives

Possible Side Effects: Resistance to or resentment of family gatherings, feelings of powerlessness, increased likelihood of future sexual or physical victimization

Of all the parental statements I discuss in this book, this is probably the one about which I feel the most strongly. I didn't want to put it first as there's a high chance of me coming off a little rant-y, and I didn't want to scare you away too soon, but this one is near and dear to my heart.

Why We Say It

It is our job as parents to socialize our children.

This is a much more difficult job than it would seem. Toddlers are perfectly capable of running into a family gathering, failing to greet a single person, calling out how ugly one family member's shoes/clothes/whatever are, asking point blank if anyone brought them presents, and then skipping out (literally) before they even get an answer to their question. Teenagers at least have the decency to walk into a room and ignore everyone quietly without looking up from their iPhones.

It's fairly obvious that part of socializing our kids is teaching them to greet people when they come into a room, to show some degree of warmth to relatives and close family friends, and to engage in at least a token effort at conversation before zooming back into their own worlds. With this goal in mind, there seems to be nothing wrong with this statement.

However, as with all the other statements in this book, the way we get this message across can have all kinds of negative consequences if we don't think it through fully.

Research Says (What They Hear)

I think this is the most important parental statement to combat because the desire to have our kids express affection to family members comes from such a good place (and is an incredibly important message to send), but the act of dictating when our kids need to have physical contact with people, even if they're a cherished member of our tribe, sets up a seriously bad precedent in a child's impressionable, little mind.

However, before we get into the crux of the issue, let me ask one pretty obvious question.

Is a Forced Hug Really a Hug?

No.

The whole point of asking our kids to give Aunt So-And-So a hug is that we want our kids to have the same feelings of fondness and affection that we do toward the people who are important in our lives. Forcing your poor offspring into an involuntary embrace with a perfume-doused octogenarian does nothing of the sort. In fact, it actually might stir up some resentment if it happens too frequently.

Similarly, you might also be making the relative in question feel uncomfortable as well. It is exactly no one's idea of a good time to wait patiently and watch a toddler tantrum unfold because a small child is that unwilling to hug you. Not really giving Aunt So-And-So the warm fuzzies, now are we?

It is perfectly acceptable to want your child to be polite, emerge briefly from their electronic devices, and greet their relatives when they see them. That isn't too much to ask. However, it's usually a better idea to let your child authentically and voluntarily choose the manner in which they do so. The more forced the situation is, the less genuine affection it usually conveys. If your children want to walk into a nursing home and fist bump their great grandpa, I'd say more power to them. They might have to teach Great Grandpa what a fist bump is first, but go for it. I'd rather get a genuine fist bump than a forced hug any day of the week.

What To Say Instead

So, now that we've briefly mentioned the importance of letting your child display affection in whatever manner they feel comfortable, let's talk about the meat of the issue: why it's a horrible, no good, very bad idea to force your child into physical contact for any reason.

The Importance of Consent

As you had probably guessed, this is going to be another section about consent.

The most common application of the concept of consent is to sexual situations in which any party has the right to say no (aka withdraw their consent) at any time, but the concept of consent has so much broader of an application than just in the bedroom or when a person starts dating.

You want your kids to understand no one is allowed to touch their body without their permission. This helps them train friends to exercise boundaries, gives them the skills and confidence necessary to ward off potential predators or child molesters, promotes proper hygiene (especially at the toddler age level when who knows what all their peers are touching before they attempt to manhandle your child), and sets them up to reap a lifetime of benefits under the idea that they have control and authority over their own person.

Childhood could potentially be a scary time because kids are littler, weaker, and less socially powerful than a majority of the people in their immediate surroundings. As parents, we want to teach kids that their body is entirely their own. No one is allowed to use their size, age, or position of authority to put your kid into an uncomfortable position. We can all agree on these ideals when they are *And kiddos need to know we support their choices.* [Crystal] discussed theoretically, but it takes a little forethought to realize that sometimes we as parents are guilty of violating them as well. Forcing a kid to kiss a relative, requiring two fighting siblings to hug it out, or any other form of (however well-meaning) coerced physical contact should be deleted from every parent's vocabulary.

It's not that forcing your kids to hug after a fight is going to land them in therapy for life. It won't. Just like if they have to suck it up and kiss Grandma Mildred's cheek every year on Easter, you aren't dooming them to a life of victimization and helplessness.

However, if you do stand up for them and tell creepy Uncle Buck that your kid doesn't have to sit in his lap if they don't feel like it but that they can show him a cool new high five that "all the cool kids are doing" will send your child an incredibly powerful message about how it's acceptable to refuse to do things that make you uncomfortable even to those you love or respect.

The Challenges of Drawing Boundaries

The act of understanding what makes you feel comfortable and uncomfortable, and then forcing other people to abide by the standards you set is called having boundaries (Knittel, 2017). Giving your children the green light to defend their body against physical contact that makes them uncomfortable begins the very essential training that will lead to them being able to maintain their own healthy boundaries later in life.

This doesn't just mean they won't tolerate attempted date rape (as so many discussions of consent would boil it down to) but enables a whole spectrum of healthy behaviors. Having healthy boundaries as an adult means they will value their own opinion, they'll be able to stand up better and more effortlessly to peer pressure, they won't tolerate abuse or disrespect even from those in positions of authority over them, and they'll be more accepting when others exercise their right to say no as well. Teaching kids that they have control over their own bodies, environments, and choices (and teaching them to extend this right to others as well) is one of the most important things we can do as parents to ensure their safety after they leave our protective bubble of influence.

Consent at All Ages

Most lessons on consent are aimed at teens who are just starting to date and college students who are just starting to date unsupervised. This is about a decade too late.

The personality your children develop and the way they act as a toddler has been statistically shown to predict their personality up to 40 years later (Blatney, Jelinek, & Osecka, 2007). By the time teens are getting ready for their first date, they have already developed (or neglected) the skill set that will allow them to confidently rebuff unwanted advances if said date decides to get frisky. By the time your kid is getting yelled at by an unreasonable boss, the kid's firmly entrenched personality will determine how handle the situation.

By the time your kid hits an actual "hot water" situation, it will be too late to rationally say it's okay to stand up for oneself. This message needs to be imparted to them early and often. Just the way we need to tell kids eight bajillion times that they need to say "thank you" when someone gives them something or to clean up their plates when they're finished eating, it is equally important that we drill into them the idea that they can say no to people who ask them to do things that make them uncomfortable.

What Aunt Ethel Has to Do with Neuroplasticity

Neuroplasticity is one of my favorite psychological concepts of all time. The concept of neuroplasticity lays down the neurological facts behind the idea that how you choose to think can have a powerful impact on your habits, long-term personality, and even the physical structure of your brain itself.

When you think of neuroplasticity, think of your brain like a field that has recently been covered by a thick covering of snow. It starts out equally challenging to take any path across the field. Then, you walk across it once. It's hard going the first time, but now there's one path (the one you already took) that's much easier than the others. You can choose to take a new path and do slightly more work in breaking it in, or you can take the path you have already taken and have a slightly easier time of it. As you keep walking across the field over and over, the paths you take frequently become easier and easier to take while the paths not used gradually get filled in by fresh snow.

The brain works the same way. The first time you utilize a thought process, such as deciding it's okay to stand up for yourself when you really don't want to give creepy Uncle Reginald the requested cheek kiss, it might be a pretty hard decision. There will be some anxiety, some hemming and hawing, and a solid measure of self-doubt. That's because it's the first time your neurons are firing in that particular pattern so they're not used to it. There's no pre-trodden path through the snow.

Then, the more you exercise a thought pattern, the easier and more intuitive it gets to do so. Your brain will actually physically change in structure, devoting more and more resources to the neural pathways you use frequently, diverting those resources away from the pathways not frequently used.[27]

This explains why people who are "mentally tough" seem to weather difficult events with ease. They have, over many challenging events of increasing magnitude, repeatedly trodden the pathways for self-calming behaviors, rational situation analysis, and looking on the bright side, all the while being careful not to walk down mental roads of self-pity, avoidance, or wallowing. In constantly choosing to think in productive ways, they have actually changed their brain chemistry to become mentally stronger in the skills they repeatedly practice. This way, when a challenge is presented, they are "mentally buff" and are therefore more prepared to handle it.

What does this have to do with forced hugs with crazy Aunt Edna?

We want our kids to be mentally strong, to develop healthy boundaries, and to have no qualms about telling people who try to put them in uncomfortable positions just where they can shove it. This doesn't happen in one parental lecture, nor does it happen instantaneously. As a parent, your job is to shepherd your kids through practice exercise after practice exercise, showing them exactly how to

---

27   This is immensely cool to my inner nerd because it means how you think is literally changing the physical structure of your body.

stand up for themselves, how to define their boundaries, and that they don't have to feel guilty for doing so.

As you give your kid repeated practice with these skills, neuroplasticity will kick in and turn those repeated practice exercises into ingrained habits and character traits. Then once your children does internalize these principles, they will automatically begin to defend their boundaries and say no to peer (and authority) pressure, and, more important, they will do so instinctively.

(i.e. Punch them in the face.) [Crystal]

Modeling and the Art of Leaning into the Awkward

So, I've hopefully convinced you to lay off the guilt trips about exchanging unsolicited hugs with relatives, but you're probably wondering what you should say to said relatives about the sudden change in protocol.

First, you can definitely warn them ahead of time not to expect forced hugs from your kids, as a heads up in advance will definitely help smooth things over. However, it can also send a much more potent message to your kids to watch you stand up to a relative on their behalf. Sure, you can talk the talk about being able to turn down physical contact if you don't want it, but when you're staring down the barrel of a familial sad puppy face it can be a different story.

Your kid needs to see you face an offended or put out relative and tell them point blank that they are owed absolutely nothing from your kid and to kindly back off. Even better, let your kid watch you model the appropriate setting of boundaries. Say no to a hug and request a handshake instead. Comment (politely) when strangers impose on your

No, my son won't wonder if I have his back. [Crystal]

personal space, and show your kids the world isn't going to think less of them for demanding that people respect their boundaries, whatever they may be. These actions will be more poignant of a message than a thousand parental lectures on consent.

Cheat Sheet

- Suggest healthy alternatives before entering a situation. If you don't want to offend your relatives, one thing I do suggest is to prep your kid with some acceptable alternatives. If you know your child isn't a hugger, arm them with the idea to suggest a high five, handshake, or fist bump before their relatives try to corner them for an awkward embrace.

- Modeling is key. Let your kids see you standing up for your own boundaries as well as defending theirs. Nothing is more powerful to a kid than watching how you handle real-life situations so seek out examples to show your kids that you can maintain healthy boundaries without being rude. (Remember, everyone gets baseline politeness, affection has to be earned and voluntarily given.)

- Teach consent skills early and often. This isn't a skill that can be taught on the fly or at the last minute. The more you bring these issues up, talk about them, and practice them, the more instinctively they will come to your children when their backs are up against a wall.

- Remember neuroplasticity. Practice, practice, practice. You want the area of your children's brains that is responsible for standing up for themselves to be as buff as possible so that when the time comes, you know they will default to strong, healthy behaviors.

Liz Bayardelle, Ph.D.

8

Win Your Game Today

Intended Use: To get your kid to do well at an upcoming sports event

Possible Side Effects: Decreased ambition, fear of failure, challenge avoidance

It makes perfect sense that when a uniform-clad kiddo walks out the door on the day of a big game, a parent naturally offers a cheer in the form of a "crush the other team today, champ" or some other good-natured encouragement. Seeing as it's a chapter in this book, you can safely assume I'm going to tell you this might not be a good idea. You would be unsurprisingly correct in this assumption, but I want to clarify a few things before I explain why you shouldn't place excessive emphasis on your kid winning a sports game.

Why We Say It

There are actually a lot of reasons parents say this one.

Most of us aren't actually thinking too hard about it. We're just wishing our kid luck and demonstrating that we do, in fact, listen when they talk and that we actually remembered that they have a game that day. No further brain cells needed.

However, there are other motivations for this particular parental nudge that do merit specific mentions.

First, Check Your Own Ego

It's very hard to parent without seeing your child as a tiny version or extension of yourself, at least to some degree. This is not bad and is completely natural.

However, many parents take the having pride in your children a step (or five) too far. And here's where it comes time for some tough talk.

If you're trying to get your child to win their game because you want to prove the superiority of your parenting, because you're making up for the fact that you weren't a good athlete as a child, or because you want to relive your glory days as a star whatever, you need to sit the heck down and close your face hole.[28]

Today's kids have an immense amount of pressure on their tiny shoulders. They already have pressure from judgmental peers, high standards from teachers, siblings to live up to, as well as the ever-looming undertaking that is the college application process. They don't need you heaping your psychological issues onto their already-full plate.

This isn't the main point of this chapter and only you can know if this applies to you, but if you think you're encouraging your kids to win for anyone's benefit other than their own you might want to consider some well-meaning silence or a supportive hug instead.

Tough talk over.

Little League Parents versus the Participation Trophy Generation

Second, I am not trying to get you to de-emphasize winning because I am a member of the "kids shouldn't keep score because it damages their fragile self-esteem" club. If you're unfamiliar with this long-standing parental debate, sit back, and grab a bag of popcorn. It's about to get real.

In the "good old days" kids would form two teams and play a game. At the end of the game, the team with the most points would be declared the winners, and the team with fewer points would be declared the losers. There would be a certain amount of gloating and/or sulking, and then everyone would go home for the night. Sounds pretty logical, right?

Alas, it could not remain that simple. Sometime in the last decade or so a new movement has emerged. This new philosophy declared that we needed to be more mindful of crushing the budding self-esteem of our precious, fragile, little flowers, especially the younger ones. This school of thought gave birth to the scoreless Little

28   Sorry, I really tried to put that one nicely, but that's the best I could do.

League game, the participation trophy, and a myriad of other practices that make "old school" Little League parents roll their eyes and bite their tongues.

While there is a shocking dearth of empirical research on the long-term benefits or detriments to a child's psychological health or future accomplishment levels, more than half of Americans solidly believe that only "winners" should get trophies (Ekins, 2014).

> *Here's a "you may suck but we love you" trophy.* [Crystal]

I am definitely with the majority here, but it's not because I want to crush the nascent self-esteem of your beautiful, little, angel child. Instead, I want to take this opportunity to present to you my love letter to failure. Before you dismiss this as bizarre, I do want to put it out there that I literally wrote my doctoral dissertation on the subject of failure[29], so I actually do know what I'm talking about.

Research Says (What They Hear)

The academic world (in which kids exist up to the age of 18) is one in which they are given all the tools and knowledge they need before they take the test. Kids begin to learn that failure is avoidable and, therefore, that success is defined as the act of avoiding failure. In their defense, this is pretty true in the academic world. Succeeding at school means avoiding failing tests, getting good grades all the time, and eventually getting that rockstar GPA that will have colleges drooling all over you.

However, in "real life" we very rarely know we're even being tested until a failure occurs, not to mention the fact that we almost never receive all the necessary information to avoid failure before it happens. In the adult world, the main measure of success is not how well we *avoid* failure, but rather in how well we *react* to it.

As stated by the inimitable J. K. Rowling in her famed Harvard commencement address, "It is impossible to live without failing at something unless you live so cautiously that you might as well not have lived at all—in which case, you fail by default" (2008).

> *I'm constantly trying to teach my mentees that failure is GOOD!* [Kristine]

Failure is not something that is avoidable, at least not outside academia. The difference between winners and losers in the adult world is how quickly a person recognizes a failure, how accurately they dissect the situation to determine what went wrong, how thoroughly they learn the necessary lessons to prevent future failures of the same ilk, and how quickly they get back on the horse to try again.

---

29   I often joke that I want to get business cards printed saying I have a Ph.D. in failure. Someday, I'm actually going to do it.

Thinking of failure from this perspective, as an unavoidable and defining hallmark of success in the real world, it becomes something we need to go out of our way to teach our children how to do well. Just like we need to teach our kids how to walk, read, study properly, and interact with other humans in a positive way, we need to teach our kids how to fail well.

> *And how not to equate failures with loss of self-worth.* [Crystal]

From this lens, it becomes almost unthinkable that we would even consider depriving kids the chance to lose at sports by giving them a participation trophy. It is good, useful, and necessary that kids lose (or fail) at sporting events. Most important, kids should be given as many opportunities to fail as humanly possible because repeated practice is the only way to get better at anything.

Mindset (Kiddie Sports Edition)

By trying to avoid failure, we paint it as something horrible, unspeakable, and shameful, something that should be avoided at any costs. This sets them up for a very unpleasant life because, as we just discussed, failure is not only unavoidable but is actually the source of a majority of the learning that takes place after one leaves the academic world.

Back in Chapter 1, we talked about the work of psychologist Carol Dweck, who looked at the difference between kids with a "fixed mindset," who saw failure as a mark that they weren't good enough and shut down after experiencing a failure, and those with a "growth mindset," who experienced a failure and took it as a challenge and opportunity for further learning. The kids with a "growth mindset" were less upset in the face of failure, had higher subsequent levels of motivation, were more likely to seek out challenging activities, and were less likely to cheat or stoop to unethical means to achieve their goals.

Knowing this, why on earth would we want to stigmatize failure as something bad or shameful for our kids? By suggesting that kids' self-esteem would be crushed by not getting a trophy at the end of every soccer game, we are subtly suggesting to them that it is somehow shameful not to get a trophy even though it's highly unlikely that even the most gifted of children will go through life winning everything they ever do.

Hiding from Failure (and Other Hallmarks of a Fixed Mindset)

What I fear will be one of the outcomes of the participation trophy movement with the most long-reaching detrimental consequences is that if kids are not indoctrinated early and often to the idea that failure is an acceptable (and expected) part of life, they will slowly begin to avoid situations in which failure is likely.

This sounds logical. We all want to avoid failure, right?

Yes, but let's take this trait to its logical conclusion. It starts out with a kid not wanting to do a sport he or she feels bad at. This isn't the biggest deal in the world, so as parents we're more than willing to allow it. However, the only way any kid ever gets good at anything is by sucking, practicing anyway, sucking less, practicing some more, becoming halfway decent, and then practicing a few thousand more hours before they're actually considered "good" at it.

So, we now have kids who avoid sports altogether because they never pushed past the initial sucking phase (aka failure) to get to the good part. Now is when neuroplasticity kicks in. They're used to ducking out of sports when things get hard, so it isn't too much of a stretch to opt out of the honors track at school, knowing they'll get better grades in the easier courses. This way they may get decent grades but probably won't want to risk being rejected from their "reach" schools so they only apply to colleges they know they'll get into. Continuing on in kind with a life of relatively safe mediocrity.

I won't take this *reductio ad absurdum* much further (although I could, and it would be depressingly bleak). You can see the general trajectory of a life lived in avoidance of failure, and it doesn't really scream "interesting, successful human being," does it?

What To Say Instead

Wrapping up my love letter to failure, I implore any loving parent to throw their kids headfirst into as many hard, challenging, and failure-prone situations as early and as often as possible. Make failure just as common in childhood as it is in the real world, even more common if you can manage it because (just like anything else) they'll need lots of practice to get good at failing well.

Nailing That First Failure

The first failure kids experience will be at a very young age on a very small scale. Maybe they lose a pretend gymnastics meet at your Mommy-and-me class. Maybe a friend doesn't want to play with them at the park. Possibly they don't score a goal in their first Little League soccer game (or first season, for that matter).

When a failure hits, you have two possible courses of action as a parent. One course makes this first failure experience out to be a horrible thing. Common, well-meaning parental responses include "Oh, I'm so sorry sweetie," "I know how upset you must be," or "That really sucks, but you'll get 'em next time." All of these responses are said with the utmost love and the goal of making your child feel better, but they send the message that failure is a negative thing that your child should be upset about now and avoid later.

Alternatively, the second and better course, treats the first failure as a "duh" moment of expected inevitability. Tell your kids that *of course* things didn't work out perfectly the first time because almost nothing ever goes perfectly the first time. Tell them that's the point of practicing. Tell them that everyone who's really great at anything absolutely sucked the first time (or the first hundred times) they tried the thing they're now awesome at doing. Tell them how Michael Jordan was cut from his high school varsity basketball team (Newsweek Special Edition, 2015). Tell them stories about your most epic flops in life.

Or Harry trying to learn how to conjure a patronus. [Crystal]

Then, tell them that the point of failing is to give you information about what to do better next time. Sit down with them and go over their game, gymnastics meet, or park date. Show them that maybe they could practice dribbling a little more, maybe they got distracted by their shiny new leotard and lost focus, maybe they shouldn't have thrown sand into everyone's hair. Then, once you've identified something tangible to work on, show them that the failure was good because now they have this valuable little knowledge nugget they didn't have before.

Most important, throw them into the same situation again as soon as you can so they learn that the world didn't end just because they did it wrong the first time. The more opportunities kids have to fail, learn, and realize that it's not actually the end of the world when it happens, the less phased they'll be by failure and the more challenging activities they'll be willing to pursue.

The Benefit of Repeated Failures

We discussed neuroplasticity in the last chapter, how your brain strengthens the neural pathways you use most frequently which, consequently, makes repeated thought patterns easier and easier to access. This is why repeated failures, handled properly and starting as early in childhood as possible, are absolutely necessary to a child's development.

The more you create opportunities to fail safely, that is on a small scale with no long-term repercussions, the more you strengthen the neural pathways that will help your kid not freak out when they aren't perfect right away, the pathways of thought that will help them see failure as a learning opportunity rather than a catastrophic road block in their life plan, and the mental habits that will help them get back up after they've been knocked to the metaphorical (or literal) ground.

Failing Well

Further, teaching children not to freak out when they fail isn't actually your only mission here. As a parent, what you should be doing is teaching them how to recognize a failure, diagnose what needs to be fixed to avoid subsequent failures, and then learn the appropriate lessons as fast as possible. So, just like any other skill you teach your kids: practice, practice, practice. This means get them in front of as many failures as possible and then helping them learn how to handle the failures productively.

High-five them when they accidentally score on their own team in their lacrosse game.[30] Give them a huge hug when they almost drown halfway down the swim lane in their first meet. Take them out for ice cream when they come in last in their soccer tournament. Then, later that night, sit them down with a big bowl of potato chips and help them create a plan for what they're going to work on next week in practice.

As you show them the process of failing well, that is, not being phased by a failure, milking it for all it's worth as a learning opportunity, and then getting back on the horse, their little sponge-like brains are going to be internalizing this pattern, and it will become more and more intuitive, turning your kids into fearless, challenge-seeking adults who aren't phased when life throws a challenge their way.

What Our Kids Actually Learn from Sports

This section was supposed to be titled "why we still force our kids to suit up at 7 a.m. on a Saturday morning even though we are 100% sure they'll never go pro", but it was a little too long to fit on the page. However, the point remains that almost all kids play some kind of sport sometime in their childhood even though only a tiny percentage of kids end up playing any time past high school, not to mention professionally. So, why do we encourage our kids to do something that has very little chance of contributing to their future career?

Surprisingly enough, a vast majority of the benefits of Little League sports have absolutely nothing to do with sports. When kids join a team, they learn how to cooperate with a group of people with whom they may or may not get along, a skill that will be infinitely useful in countless hellish workplaces to come. Committing to a team on a long-term basis teaches kids staying power and how to care about a goal that involves more than just themselves. Working under a coach teaches them how to receive feedback and use it to make yourself better. And yes, sports give kids a lot of opportunity to lose and fail until they can do so gracefully.

Most important, sports provide kids with a perfect opportunity to start at the beginning (where they absolutely suck at something), diagnose their own weaknesses, utilize their resources (e.g. coaches, teammates, etc.) to help themselves improve, and keep working and practicing until they reach a potential goal. Yes, your child isn't likely to become the next Lebron James or Misty Copeland, but that doesn't mean that sports aren't going to massively benefit your child's personality and skill development.

---

30   Yes, I did actually do this one as a child, thank you very much.

So, Is It Bad to Focus on Winning, Then?

Of course not. I'm definitely not saying you should want your kids to lose or not try to help them to win. They should, however, be *prepared* for a potential loss because a childhood without any kind of failure is pretty unlikely, but you should definitely want your kid to win, to want to win, and to try their damnedest to come out on top.

However (and a fairly large however), there are much more important things to focus on than just winning for the sake of winning.

Back in Chapter 2, we talked about lead measures and lag measures. Basically, *lag measures* are things that happen after an action has already taken place. Winning a game happens after the play has already concluded. You get a grade after it is already too late to change how you studied for the test. These are lag measures because they lag after the determining actions.

In contrast, *lead measures* are things that happen before the actions that determine a goal take place. Management psychologists highly suggest focusing more energy on lead metrics because they impact things they can actually control, where lag metrics occur after the time for helpful action has already passed. It's the same with parenting. Telling your kid to win is a lag metric. It's a great goal, but by the time they've won or lost there's really not much they can do about it.

Instead, try refocusing your children's attention on lead metrics, that is things they have actual control over. Instead of telling them to win their game, try reminding them to keep their guide arm up when they go to hit the ball, that they keep their toes pointed when they go for that handstand at the end of their routine, or that they remember to stay on their toes when they're on defense. Does it take a little more detailed knowledge on your part? Yes, but since when is it a bad thing to be more knowledgeable about your kids' lives? The more you can help your kid focus on things like form, technique, effort, learning, and other process-driven goals, not only the more will they learn and improve but also the more winning the game will take care of itself.

Cheat Sheet

We've discussed a lot in this chapter, from fixed versus growth mindsets, to neuroplasticity, to my love affair with failure. Overall, there are two different and completely separate points you need to learn from this chapter:

1. Aiming to win is good, but losing should not be the end of the world.

2. Place more emphasis on controllable, process-driven goals than just the endgame of winning.

If you can convey both of these messages to your offspring, you're going to create pretty awesome kids. Here's how:

- Get your ego out of the way. If you're telling your kid to win because it helps bolster your self-esteem as a super parent, quit it right now. Sit down, and shut up. You had your time, and now it's about them.

- Normalize failure. The more you convey the message that failure is a normal, acceptable, and even beneficial feature of life, the less likely your kids are to freak out when they aren't perfect the first time. Failure is just feedback. You don't want timid, little kids who are afraid to try new things for fear of failing.

- Create as many opportunities as you can for your child to fail. The more kids fail, the more they learn that it's not the end of the world when they do. Not only does this take a psychological load of pressure off their shoulders, it frees them up to try challenging things without being turned off by the higher likelihood of failure.

- Teach your child to fail productively. Failing productively simply means that you harness your failures to give yourself some kind of learning, progress, or growth. A failure you don't learn from is actually a bad thing. This isn't because your kid failed but because they missed an opportunity to learn or improve themselves. Whenever your kids fail, help them milk the failure for every ounce of personal growth they can muster.

- Stress process-driven, lead measures, rather than just winning for the sake of winning. Help your kid find the specific behaviors that will lead to winning. Instead of focusing on getting the eventual win, suggest focusing on technique, effort, focus, or other controllable behaviors that will lead toward the eventual outcome of winning.

- Appreciate all the life-lessons your kids are getting from sports regardless of the final outcome of the game. Kids learn patience, teamwork, cooperation, social skills, how to deal with authority figures, how to take feedback, how to self-diagnose and work to improve their own skills, and many other important skills. Keep in mind the big picture rather than just the outcome of one sports match.

Finish Your Homework

DOCTOR'S WARNING

Intended Use: To get your kids to finish their homework sometime this century

Possible Side Effects: Low quality work, poor retention, less learning, more negative sentiment towards homework, less initiative taken for their own learning

Alright, this chick is officially off her rocker. What on God's green earth could possibly be wrong with telling your kids to finish their homework?[31]

Why We Say It

First, let me say I'm definitely guilty of this one. On more than one occasion. Okay, fine! I say this every darn day. There is absolutely nothing wrong with you as a parent for wanting your kids to stop messing around and do their freaking homework

 *Even when "homework" is stuff he loves doing!* [Kristine]

---

31   If that's even possible.

already. I wish for homework to be completed without a fight almost as often as I wish for an extra hour of sleep.

However, that doesn't mean it's not a genuinely dangerous thing to say. As with most of the other statements in this book, there isn't too much wrong with the sentiment behind telling your kids to finish their homework, but there are a number of really damaging messages that sneak in the door with this seemingly innocuous request.

Research Says (What They Hear)

Here's a list of all the things your kid hears when you shout "finish your homework" over your shoulder while trying to balance your cell phone on your ear to take a work call while rocking a baby on one hip and stirring a pot of pasta with the other hand.[32] These misapprehensions include:

- Homework is a negative event (like broccoli or cleaning your room) that should be dealt with before you can do more enjoyable things.

- Homework should be done as quickly as possible.

- The goal of homework is to be done with homework.

- If you finish all your homework every day, you will succeed in school.

- If you know how to do your homework, you will do fine on any upcoming tests.

Wait, I didn't say any of that! No, my dear, you didn't say it with your mouth, but it's definitely still what your kiddos heard. It's kind of like when you say "no," and they hear "go ask your father because he's incapable of saying no to his perfect little angel baby." It's the underlying message that matters even if it's not coming from the specific words you say.

So, let's unpack each of the underlying messages that your kids hear when you say "finish your homework" on a voyage to understand how to get the little buggers to finish their homework in a way that doesn't turn around and bite you on your amply postpartum booty (or your sympathy baby belly, for the dads in the crowd).

Homework Isn't a Punishment

This is a very common preconception that almost all kids feel at some point in time in their academic careers.

Childhood is full of a million different fun things you can do, and your kid wants to do all of them.[33] The problem is that school takes up a large portion of their days. The last thing kids want to do when they get home from eight hours of academic

---

32   Or is that just me? No? Good. Multitaskers assemble!

33   Often at the same time.

drudgery (in their opinion, at least) is do more schoolwork. Consequently, they either rush through it first thing when they get home to get it out of the way (if you're killing it at the parenting thing), or they do it as quickly as possible on the bus ride to school the morning of (if you're having a hard week and are really just grateful their socks match each other).

Either way, homework is commonly viewed as the bane of a child's existence, a viewpoint which is gleefully perpetrated by friends, children's cartoons and TV shows, adults who don't know better,[34] and sometimes even their teachers themselves. But, alas, homework is *not* just a necessary evil sent by vengeful teachers who are out to ruin your kid's spare time.

In reality, homework is a tool. The point of homework is that it can be used to make kids understand more than teachers can teach in one 48-minute class period or to give kids extra practice on what was taught. It's not a punishment or a mindless chore, it's just a tool. Nothing more, nothing less.

With this in mind, you can see that the problem here isn't that you need your kids to love doing homework, but that you need them to see that its purpose is to help them learn more and learn better, not just to rob them of their rightfully earned weekday afternoons.

Speed Usually Means Low Quality and Lower Retention

So, why does it matter how your kids think of homework? It matters because it changes their mindset as they do it.

If your kid does any task as fast as they possibly can, they're probably going to do it with the lowest quality possible to still count as "accomplishing" the task. Just as cleaning their room as fast as possible leads to things hastily shoved in drawers and under beds, doing homework as fast as possible leads to missed answers, shortcuts taken, and very little learning actually accrued. You want kids to actually pay attention to what they're doing in their homework because research shows that not repeating a learning experience (like learning something once in class and then refreshing themselves while doing homework) seriously hampers long-term retention of the material (Karpicke & Roediger, 2006).

Basically, if your kids are doing their academic impression of Dale Earnhardt when they sit down at their desk, you can almost guarantee that they aren't getting very much out of it, learning wise.

This is especially unfortunate because if homework's purpose is to be a tool of learning, doing it so quickly that you guarantee no real learning is taking place deprives it of its purpose and reduces it to just a waste of your kid's time and energy. Whatever you tell your kid about homework, you should not stress speed as a goal.

I'll be honest, I am not a fan of any busy work. [Crystal]

---

34   You know, the ones who haven't read this book.

Now, before you decide this book would be better kindling than reading material or start screaming into the pages about how long your little procrastinator would take to do his or her homework if you didn't stress speed as a goal, let me clarify that you can stress many other things which will greatly reduce their overall homework time. You just shouldn't overtly or explicitly encourage speed. [35]

Instead of using phrases like "hurry up," "get it done," "as soon as possible," or "before dinner," try stressing doing something in one sitting, doing it without getting distracted, or getting started as fast as possible. When you tell your kids to do their homework quickly, you don't actually want them to rush through it. You just want them to do it without messing around for 43 minutes before starting in the guise of "getting organized" or stopping every other problem to retie their shoes, go get a snack, or play a quick game on their iPad.

If your kids actually came home, got started without procrastinating, and then worked with focus and without distraction until they were finished with their homework, you probably wouldn't care if it took them all night. You'd probably be proud if it did. Your seeming emphasis on speed really isn't related to speed, but rather a lack of procrastination or loss of focus. If you need to rush your kids along, try focusing on their negative study behaviors (procrastination, stalling, pausing to look at butterflies, etc.) instead of rushing them through the actual work itself.

Aim for the Right Goals

Finishing homework fast is only one of many times in a kid's academic career where they are funneled toward the wrong goals. As a parent, your job is to look past the temporary, quick wins and try to focus your kid on the longer-term goal.

In the instance of doing homework, you have the challenging job of overcoming the societal perception that homework is a miserable daily exercise that has to be endured and completed as fast as possible and convincing your children to utilize it as the tool it is. Try to get them in the mindset of using the homework as a practice for their upcoming tests. When a problem is hard for them, it's an indication that they need to study that area more thoroughly, while easy problems for them indicate that they have probably mastered that subject.

A Very Important (Yet Slightly-Less-Than-Related) Point

A similar dynamic is present when it comes to school itself. The academic world focuses a great deal of attention on test grades, report cards, GPA's, college acceptances, and other things

> *I was nearly a 4.0 student... and retained very little.* [Kristine]

---

[35]   Also shouting at inanimate objects is the kind of behavior that garners really strange looks from those around you. Rule number one of parenting is to attempt to appear sane at all times even though we all know parenthood and sanity have a very hard time residing in the same body.

that, when you really think about it, don't exactly measure the skills kids will need later in life.

Think of it this way, a kid can easily cram for a test the day before, get an A on the test, then have completely forgotten all of the subject matter by the same time the next week. This kid is technically getting good grades but not really learning very much except for how to cram for academic tests.

College calculus: I can confirm there's a 0% retention rate. [Crystal]

Contrast this with a kid who studies slowly over time, trying to internalize the material rather than just passing the test. This kid will probably also do well on the test but will also know the material better when it comes to the cumulative final at the end of the semester, two years later when volunteering as a peer tutor for younger kids, or in 20 years when his or her own child holds out what is very likely the same dang math book, looking for help.

These latter children will also have the material at their disposal when they need it in the course of their career as an adult which, even though it is always somehow lost in translation, is the whole darn point of the educational system. School is supposed to prepare kids for real life. Cramming for test after test in order to get a 4.0 GPA in things you don't remember may get your kid that $0.11 piece of paper that says they went to a great college,[36] but it won't give them the skills they need once they finally get out into the real world.

Doing their English homework to get it done fast may get your kid full credit, but doing it thoroughly and for comprehension will get them the writing skills that will help them write anything from cover letters to amicus briefs. Cramming for that test may still get them the grade but studying thoroughly over time with the goal of actually internalizing the material will set them up to be a world-class mind rather than just the graduate of a name brand college.

Basically, even with all the focus on and talk about speed, grades, and GPA's, try to keep your eye on actual learning and train your child to do the same. It will put them leagues apart when they actually join the workforce.

What To Say Instead

After that slight detour, let's finally get to what you should actually be saying to your kiddos in place of "finish your homework."

When your child is just starting elementary school, they will most likely be given mind-numbingly boring homework. This is usually intentional as it would be incredibly poor manners for the educational system to attempt to break

And this is why we learn to hate homework. [Crystal]

---

36   Otherwise known as a diploma.

their tiny spirits so young.[37] Well, that and the fact that they're really just trying to accustom kids to the act of doing homework.

Then, at some point in time between first grade and their third year of law school, some parts of their homework begin to become challenging. This is the point at which finishing homework becomes even trickier. You now have to spend even longer trying to figure out things that you don't understand, not just regurgitating things and practicing stuff you could do in your sleep. It is at this point that your kid will become even more jubilant the second their homework is completed because now it is not only boring but also falls somewhere on the spectrum between mildly frustrating and downright painful.

The tricky part is that right when homework gets harder and kids get even more glad to be done with it each afternoon is when they start needing to do more work to supplement their mandatory homework.

What? Voluntary homework? Blasphemy!

Nope! Welcome to academics!

Remember how we talked about homework just being a tool? Well, one of the uses of this tool is to diagnose what areas need more help and what areas your kids know like the back of their hand. This means that, when your kids struggle with a math problem, when they can't quite conjugate the past tense form of French verbs, when they can't remember all the key players in the first World War, that's exactly when they need to use their homework to tell them where to direct some extra work.

A student who is just doing their homework to get it done (or the kid who crams the night before the test) can just stop at the bare minimum. However, now your kids are going to be among the golden few who actually aim to learn, master, and internalize the subject material. This means that when they stumble while doing a word problem in their math homework, instead of thanking God when it's over, they will start paging through their book to find more word problems like that one so they can practice them until it's easy. A challenging worksheet in English doesn't merit an extra half hour of video games in celebration, it means they'll grab their handy-dandy index cards and start making up flashcards for the words they didn't know.

You may think that this is unrealistic to ask of a kid or that this is training behaviors only nerds would actually use. This couldn't be farther from the truth. It might sound weird for a student to voluntarily seek out extra work, but remember that the main purpose of educating a child is to prepare them for the real world. One of the key predictors of success in the workplace is a person's ability to be proactive and show initiative in taking on tasks above and beyond their job description (Campbell, 2000). Learning how to find your own areas of weakness and seek out

---

37   In modern schools, they now try to wait until at least third grade for the ceremonial crushing of the spirits.

avenues of improving them, even if it means extra work, will help your child more than calculus (or even getting straight A's in calculus) ever could.

Diagnosing Academic Needs

Since this is such a necessary skill both in the academic world and later in life, I wanted to include a quick discussion of how to teach your child to diagnose their own academic needs.

If your child is failing a class (or even getting a B),[38] there's a pretty solid chance he or she doesn't know why. Yes, on rare, clear-cut occasions it's for something obvious like refusing to dress out for gym class or repeatedly not turning in your math homework. However, most of the time your kid probably honestly doesn't know how to do better.

Hermiones unite! [Crystal]

In their defense, if your children are going to class, paying attention, and completing all their homework assignments, they're probably not getting a lot of troubleshooting advice from their teachers as to what to do if they still aren't understanding the material (or getting the grade they want). They could always ask the teacher what they could do to improve their grades, but even this requires a certain amount of proactivity that isn't intuitive to most kids, especially in a world where teachers are thought of as intimidating or difficult to approach authority figures, even more so when you feel like a bad kid for getting less than stellar grades.

It will most likely fall on you as the parent to teach your kid how to diagnose their own academic needs and find ways to improve themselves. This includes things like

- looking over their homework and tests to see what types of things they repeatedly get wrong;
- mapping out the subjects, topics, or concepts with which they're struggling;
- finding extra practice problems using their course resources (textbooks, extra worksheets, websites, etc.);
- seeking out extra help or advice from teachers; and
- testing out different study strategies (rereading the book, making flashcards, creating study guides, forming peer study groups, finding a tutor, etc.).

While this list is by no means all-inclusive, it should give you an idea of the type of things you should be doing with your kids when they need to improve their grades.

---

38 Which in some people's books is failing. These are my people.

Even more important than raising a bad grade, when your kid exercises these particular academic muscles, they're learning how to self-diagnose weaknesses, analyze their options, and create a path for self-improvement. This is a skill that will be far more useful in the long-term than anything your kids actually learn in school.

This is particularly true for kiddos with learning differences. [Crystal]

Cheat Sheet

- Fight against the idea that homework is punishment. The world is going to be against you on this one, but try to be the lone clarion voice in your child's head advocating the purpose of homework: teaching more than can fit into class time, helping reinforce what was learned, practicing for the test, and diagnosing what isn't understood yet.

- Focus on eliminating bad habits, not rushing good ones. When you tell your kids to finish their homework, what you probably mean is "stop messing around and get to it already". Make sure you aim your efforts toward curtailing procrastination, killing distractions, and increasing focus, rather than just rushing your kids' work.

- Teach them to focus on actual learning, not just test prep. It's insanely tempting to just go for the A even if you don't really learn the material. Don't let your kiddo fall into this trap. More than just getting them the grade, teaching them the thought process of going into a situation for what you can learn from it will help them toward success in every venture they try and will make their failures survivable (and even productive).

- Teach them to use homework to diagnose their weaknesses. Homework isn't just something to be suffered through. Teach them to use it to predict where they'd do poorly if the test were today.

- Help them find ways to improve said weaknesses even if it means extra homework. Sometimes the only way to learn the material or get a good grade[39] will be to do more work than is assigned. Get this into your child's head early. Homework is the minimum they should do. Study time, extra practice problems, or additional research are good, helpful, and necessary when they find something they haven't quite mastered yet.

---

39   Again, these are not the same thing.

10

Don't Hit

Intended Use: To keep your child from turning into a violent sociopath

Possible Side Effects: Increased likelihood of being bullied, reluctance to defend themselves, and most likely hitting anyway

As the mom of a ridiculously overactive toddler, this one gets a lot of action in our house.

When I say "overactive," I don't mean runs around the house or talks too loudly. I mean attempts to do flips off of the couch to land on the dog. I mean runs at you full speed from behind because she's realized if she gets her shoulder in the crook of your knee juuuuuust right, you'll drop like a sack of potatoes. I mean a 4-year-old who was play fighting with Dad and, after he faked getting hit and dropped to the ground, immediately and instinctively started attempting to kick him in the head.

I love my daughter more than I ever thought it was possible to love another human being, but the girl's a darn menace.

Why We Say It

Inevitably at least once a day (or hour), I have to tell her not to hit. Don't hit your brother (who is already a target at two months of age), don't hit the dog (who is usually asleep when this is going on), don't hit yourself (because she's apparently an equal opportunity sadist). I sometimes feel like I spend more time supervising violence than anyone who didn't elect to pursue a career in the WWF. However, I felt it was important to include this chapter in the book because there are several key times when kids should feel free to hit and know they won't get in trouble if they do so.

Research Says (What They Hear)

While it is definitely a fantastic idea for your kid not to go around punching people willy-nilly,[40] there are actually some really damaging messages that get sent to kids when you tell them never to hit.

Turn the Other Cheek is a Metaphor

Let me start off with a little of my backstory. I went to Sunday School every Sunday since before I can remember, and the week after I graduated from Sunday School (which happens at age 20 in our church) I began *teaching* Sunday School. I can proudly claim the "good Christian girl" moniker, but I want to make it very clear to anyone who will listen my opinion that certain parts of the Bible are not meant to be taken literally.

Just as it's not a sin to wear two different types of fabric in the same garment[41] and it's super frowned upon to sell your daughter into slavery[42], I personally think that there is some serious grey area in the whole "turn the other cheek."

I'm by no means claiming to be a Biblical scholar, but, in my opinion, the concept of turning the other cheek is supposed to discourage people from responding in kind when someone does something bad to you. On a practical level, this stops the development of arguments or feuds that go on forever because one wrong is paid back in kind, back and forth, ad infinitum. On a more theoretical level, I consider it a reminder that we have the option of taking the high road. When someone does something bad to us, it might be a smarter choice to brush it off and move on than making sure they pay proportionately for what they did to us.

However, kids do not operate on a theoretical level. As unfortunately happens with so many children, I was bullied as a kid, and I can say from experience that a little less turning the other cheek and a little more setting boundaries about what

---

40   This is, of course, a technical term for "without reason or thought." Sorry if my erudite vocabulary is confusing.

41   Leviticus 19:19 says "...neither shall a garment mingled of linen and woolen come upon thee."

42   Exodus 21:7 says "When a man sells his daughter as a slave, she will not be freed at the end of six years as the men are."

liberties other kids were allowed to take with my body would have benefitted me in every conceivable way.

I'm not condoning violence, brawling, or physical confrontations (unless absolutely necessary), but we need to make it more clear to our kids which circumstances mean they are completely allowed (and even encouraged) to defend themselves. I want my kids (of both genders) to be peaceful, rational beings who take the high road and never resort to violence unless absolutely necessary. That being said, I want to know with 100% surety that a quick and powerful right hook awaits anyone who thinks it's okay to put their hands on my kids' bodies without their permission. I only advocate physical self-defense as a last resort, once all verbal and peaceful alternatives have been exhausted, but kids need to feel comfortable enough defending themselves that they can do it without hesitation in an emergency.

Stranger Danger Is Absolute B.S.

One of the worst PSAs that ever achieved widespread popularity was the "stranger danger" campaign of the 1980's. The reason this policy was so horribly damaging is that, according to FBI statistics, only 0.1% of missing children are actually abducted by strangers (Allen, 2019). A vast majority of kidnappings (as well as child abuse, both violent and sexual) occurs at the hands of a family member or close friend.

You should definitely prepare your children to scream as loud as they can, aim for the eyes, and fight to stay in view of as many witnesses as possible if someone tries to grab them in a public area. However, it is insanely unlikely that this will ever happen.

The education that your child is (unfortunately) far more likely to need is what to do if creepy Uncle Bob does something that makes them feel uncomfortable after everyone finishes Thanksgiving lunch. Fighting back is a logical response when you are violently assaulted or forcefully abducted by a stranger, but it's most likely to be the last thing on your child's mind when they're around someone they trust or someone they've known their whole lives.

This is the most important conversation you need to have with them.

What To Say Instead

Consent is the concept that no one can touch your body without your permission. This is often used in a sexual connotation, but (as we discussed in a previous chapter) it encompasses a much broader range of behavior.

Kids need to have it drilled into their head that they have the right and the duty to protect themselves however they want if anyone ever does anything that makes them feel uncomfortable. Sometimes it *is* okay to hit.

Little kids need to be told that it's okay to try to run away or even fight back physically if someone asks them to do something they aren't comfortable doing or tries to touch them in a way they don't like. They need to know it doesn't matter if that person is a friend or relative. They need to know it doesn't matter if that person is a grown up. They need to know they aren't going to get in trouble for defending themselves even if that person says otherwise.

Kids are preprogrammed to trust adults and to try to please them, especially when it comes to the adults who are closest to them, so the idea of defending themselves against these trusted people is not always instinctive. They need to know that bad guys don't always look like bad guys. They have to be 100% sure they won't get in trouble with you for getting out of an uncomfortable situation (even if it turns out to have been a false alarm, but they were uncomfortable at the time).

Consent 2.0: Teenage Edition

This is important for little kids, but it's equally necessary (if not more so) for older kids and teens. Once your kids are in their teenage years, they have to apply the principles of consent you've been teaching them all along to a whole new realm of life: dating.

This is way harder for a teen to understand than for a toddler because toddlers never want to be in the types of uncomfortable situations that would merit physical self-defense. It's more complicated for teens. Situations where a teen will need to say no (and enforce it) are usually times where they've happily said yes to 19 things (not all of which a parent would necessarily approve of) but then they reach a point where they're no longer okay or comfortable with the 20th activity that is suggested. For example, a teen could agree to sneaking out, agree to driving down a dirt road, and agree to making out with a date, but then desire to stop when the date wants to take things farther. This is a tricky situation for them to be in.

In my opinion, the most important thing for teens to know about consent is that you can say no at any time, even if you previously said yes. The most appropriate metaphor I've ever heard for this was a British cartoon that likened consent to offering someone a cup of tea.[43] If you have 2 minutes and 50 seconds to spare, I would highly recommend you watch *Seconded!* [Crystal] the whole thing. It's as hilarious as it is spot on.

Basically this metaphor likens sexual consent to offering someone a cup of tea and goes through all the situations in which it's unacceptable to force someone to drink tea, including when they've previously wanted you to make them tea but don't currently want tea, when they're unconscious, when they asked for tea but then changed their mind, or when they started drinking a cup of tea but decided they don't want to drink any more tea.

---

43   You can watch this video at https://www.good.is/articles/consent-tea-dinosaur-pirate.

I love the tea metaphor, but however you choose to communicate it, your kids should hear about consent. They should hear about it from you. They should hear about it more than once. And they should hear that it's okay to react with physical force if someone doesn't obey their wishes about their own bodies.

Cheat Sheet

On this one, I have a few simple pieces of advice for conveying the ample grey area that comes with this topic in a way that even toddlers can understand.

- Let toddlers work out excess energy (that can often manifest itself as hitting) in a productive way. As evidenced by my Tasmanian toddlernado, toddlers and small children often hit because they just have so much darn energy they can't help themselves. Work out acceptable ways for them to work out this energy and verbally clarify that they can't hit in that situation because it's only acceptable to hit when you're defending yourself. You can even let them "practice" on a pillow bad guy. (Cardio for the tiny and a teaching moment all in one.)

- Make sure you teach your kids a clear, easy-to-understand rule for when it's okay to defend themselves physically. In our house, we went with "first you use your words, then you try to get away, then you use your fists". Even our 4-year-old has heard this so much that she can repeat this rule back to you, usually in an incredibly bored tone of voice. A complicated rule won't work here; it needs to be short and simple enough for a toddler to understand (even if your kids are in high school). They'll need to apply this litmus test in a hurry when they're in an emergency situation so it has to be quick and uncomplicated.

Have the conversation more than once. Your kids will never remember something you tell them only once. Anything you teach them has to be repeated multiple times and in multiple situations in order for them to remember and be able to apply it. We make sure we talk about this rule when she watches movies where people fight, when she tells us stories about things that happen at school, and pretty much any other time I can work it into conversation.

- Let them actually practice. Just like kids can't do math, throw a ball, or do pretty much anything else without practicing a million times first, kids won't be able to use force in a smart way without trying it out first. Every once in a while, play fight with them. Grab a pad or a pillow and teach them how to punch. Teach them what body parts to aim at in an emergency. Let them practice both the physical skills and the decision-making skills to tell when they should or shouldn't use physical force (see the next bullet on consent). If you don't talk about it, they'll never know. Normalize this to the extent where it's not a big, scary mystery, and they'll be a lot better off.

- Work conversations about consent into everyday life. Whether you have a toddler or a teenager, make sure you work the concept of consent into your everyday life. This could be when you're watching a movie, when relatives come over and demand hugs at Thanksgiving, when they're talking about their friends, or even with you. Let them know all the important concepts like it being okay for them to say no even when:

  - ...It's someone you know.

  - ...It's something you said yes to at first or on a previous occasion.

  - ...You don't want to be rude.

  - ...You still want the person to like you afterward.

  - ...You aren't sure if you should be uncomfortable.

11

Sit Still

Intended Use: To get your child to stop wreaking havoc like a tiny Tasmanian devil

Possible Side Effects: Decreased learning and skill-building, lower self-control, frustration (for them and for you), childhood obesity

Yes, I start every chapter with the disclaimer that this is something that I either say or am tempted to say to my own kiddos at least once a day.[44] This isn't to discredit my point but to illustrate that these are all quite valid desires for parents to have. It's normal for parents to want their kids to get good grades, greet their relatives at family functions, and eat their dang vegetables. These are all perfectly normal parental desires for us to have.

There is no parental desire more normal or more common than the wish for our kids to just sit still. Seriously. Must you vibrate at the dinner table? Why do you have to do laps around the car before I buckle you in? Is it absolutely necessary for

---

44   Okay, fine, every hour on the hour and sometimes many times in between.

you to kangaroo hop buck naked to the shower, or are we celebrating some kind of tribal holiday of which I was not informed?[45]

Kids sometimes possess what I can only refer to as a truly demonic level of energy. My husband and I joke that the only thing our three kids have in common is that sleep is the enemy. I bet your child agrees with them.[46]

> *Nope, for mine it's "sleep is for the weak."* [Crystal]

Unfortunately, if you take a step back from your overwhelmed and under-slept perspective as a parent and look at your child's behavior from a macrospective perspective,[47] you'll be forced to begrudgingly accept that their seemingly boundless energy is actually a good thing.

According to the CDC (Hales et al., 2017), almost 20% of children and adolescents are clinically obese, it's getting harder and harder for parents to herd their kids away from their screened devices and out onto the sports field or into the park,[48] and I'll bet you a full night of babysitting that you would give anything for a burst of that kind of energy when it's 11 p.m. and you're trying to crank out some work after you've successfully hoodwinked the progeny into an unwilling state of unconsciousness for the night.

> *Oh yes, the bleary eyed second shift.* [Crystal]

Your kid's energy is actually a really good thing, it just needs to be channeled into endeavors that don't make you check the clock at 8:37 in the morning to see if it's bedtime yet.

No, You're Not Imagining It (aka Why Kids Literally Can't Hold Still)

If it helps, you aren't making it up. There is actual scientific research that compared the physiological composition of kids to that of untrained adults and to that of adult athletes, and the kids kicked the adults' butts in both categories (Birat et al., 2018). Seriously, when compared to adult athletes, children had higher energy levels, more fatigue-resistant muscles, and a quicker recovery time from high-intensity exercise than did well-trained adult athletes. You aren't going crazy, your kid literally can (and will) run circles around you.

> *Usually while carrying something sticky and easy to spill.* [Crystal]

In this study, results on a test involving two closely consecutive sprints on a bicycle showed that untrained adults' performance decreased by 51.8% after the first sprint, that of adult athletes fell by 41.8%, and children's output only went down by 35.2%. When you take your kid to the park, they run around like the Tazmanian devil for an hour and a half, and you're the one who comes back exhausted, just re-

---

45   We are not. I checked.

46   If not, you can most certainly bite me.

47   Say that ten times fast.

48   Heck or just into the front yard to experiment with breathing fresh air for a few minutes.

member this study. Your kid isn't some freakishly energetic mutation of the laws of nature; *all* children are freakishly energetic mutations of the laws of nature.

Feel better now?

Play Is Important

Usually children's excess energy is directed at being playful. While it may seem that skipping around the house wearing soccer cleats, a princess dress, and a bicycle helmet while having conversations with tiny monsters that only your child can see might not be the most productive use of your child's time, you'd be surprised that your kid is actually deriving a great deal of psychological and developmental learning from the behavior that, were you to emulate it, would make you look like you just went off your meds in a big way.

Like making me hop around the house to avoid "lava"? [Crystal]

The simple act of playing as a child has positive long-term effects on your child's self-control, emotional abilities, brain development, socialization, representational abilities, cognitive abilities, language skills, and overall levels of creativity and imagination (Bettelheim, 1987). Physical play increases hand-eye coordination and builds strength and endurance (Whitebread et al., 2012). Play with other children increases your child's leadership skills, self-advocacy skills, ability to participate productively in a group, and overall social confidence (Milteer & Ginsburg, 2012). Play with objects increases perseverance and a positive attitude toward challenges, while rough and tumble play helps kids control aggression and build social and emotional skills (ibid.).

So, instead of rolling your eyes next time your little psychopath starts running around with socks on both hands and blue medical gloves on both feet like some kind of satanic, Martian duck, challenging all your floor lamps to duels with a Styrofoam sword,[49] try to remember that your little tyke is actually learning important skills for later in life. As my mom always said, play is a child's work.

Why You Say It

Now that we've established that your kid actually is unnaturally energetic, we can move on to an even more unnerving fact: it's not actually their energy that drives you crazy. In fact, you don't actually mind your child's energy. You actually love your child's energy. Now, before you use this book as kindling, let me explain why.

The simple fact that your child has energy is neither good nor bad. What your child chooses to *do* with that energy is what drives you crazy. There are very few parental moments prouder than watching your toddler swing across the monkey bars

---

49 True story. Not a made up scenario in the slightest. I have pictures to prove it.

way earlier than their age should permit, seeing your elementary schooler zoom around on the soccer field during their first Little League game, or watching an older child playing their heart out after they finally find "their" sport, which they love passionately and would do 24/7 if you let them.

All of these moments involve a crazy amount of energy on your child's behalf, and they make a parent's heart swell with joy. This is proof that it's not actually your child's energy that bothers you, it's the way they channel it. Basically, you don't mind that they're energetic. You do mind that they use that energy to run around your living room in circles shout singing the (87% incorrect) lyrics to *Twinkle, Twinkle, Little Star* at the top of their lungs while beating the dog over the head with an empty wrapping paper tube.[50]

> *Sounds about right, except mine hits me.* [Crystal]

So, if you can admit that it's not actually their energy that bugs you, the act of telling them to sit still starts to make a lot less sense. If it isn't bad for them to be energetic, forcing them to exercise what little discipline they possess to vibrate uncomfortably in their chairs seems a little like fighting a losing battle. And for those of us with children (especially toddlers), you know you only get to win a very finite number of battles. Spending them on curtailing your child's scientifically proven fount of boundless energy seems less and less like a good idea.

Research Says (What They Hear)

Sometimes, you really are going to need your child to sit still.

If you're at a rare sit-down dinner with your extended family, attempting to take family photos, or trying to get your kids through a close friend's wedding without causing a scene, the goal really is for your progeny to sit still and be quiet.

As you know, this is going to be challenging, but it is possible. Each kid is their own unique little snowflake when it comes to the exact sequence of tricks, bribery, and preparation that will get them to sit still, but I can give you a list of things that you can try out to see if they help increase the odds that your progeny will hold still long enough not to embarrass you in public.

- Before an event that requires sitting still, give your kiddo(s) some unstructured run around time at a park, empty field, or even your driveway. Let them get as many of their zoomies out before they get all clean and dressed.

- Bring at least three back-up plans as to how to entertain them. (Seriously, I roll three deep.) When I had to sit through a wedding with my then one-year-old, we brought my phone, baby toys, and the keychain I never let her play with. In the end, she still exhausted all

---

50 Otherwise known as "Friday night" in our house.

three options and ended up going through my wallet before the vows even started.

- When in doubt, bring lollipops. They're fairly unobtrusive, they aren't too crazy caloric, usually no one thinks twice of a kid with a lollipop (as opposed to chocolate, which they always seem to end up wearing), and it gives them something to do that also magically requires them to have their mouths shut.

- Pregame the event with some conversation about what is and isn't acceptable behavior. Anticipate things they might experience (e.g. boredom, restlessness, twitchiness, a desire to run around setting things on fire, etc.) and present them with acceptable strategies to combat these upcoming challenges. This way they're mentally prepared for what will be expected of them, and you have already established a vocabulary to use when you reprimand them later.

> *Until the sugar high...enter my ping pong ball impersonator.* [Kristine]

- Bribery. Seriously. I know it seems totally contradictory to everything I've said so far, but sometimes you have to pull out all the stops. Bribery definitely shouldn't be an everyday thing, but it's okay to pull out the big guns for the very special occasions for which you just have to make it work.[51] Promise them a special surprise: picking that night's dinner, a fun outing, or something else you can promise to them if they're good. You can also threaten to take this away if they start to act up, but remember that the number one sin in parenting is threatening to take something away and then not being able to do it. The act of issuing an empty threat loses you all your "parental street cred" with your kid and ensures they never take your word quite as seriously again.

While you might not be able to anticipate every situation, a little forethought can help you get through the infrequent one-off situations in which your kids actually do need to sit still and be quiet.

What To Say Instead

---

51   Yes, you should be hearing Tim Gunn's voice in your head.

Despite the previous section, a much larger majority of the time what you really want when you tell your child to sit still is for them to stop behaving like someone gave Red Bull to an orangutan. Running around? Fine and dandy. Running around with tap shoes trying to kick off each wall in the house as you turn the corner?[52] Hard pass.

So, if your goal isn't to induce actual stillness, then what should it be?

I would say the biggest win would be to teach our kids how to channel themselves into a positive or productive activity when they feel an extra wave of energy coming on. However, I would happily take it if they just listened to us when we tried to direct them into a more productive activity than covering their toys a bottle of lotion they found on a shelf you didn't think they could reach.[53]

Remind me to send you pictures of Powdergate. [Crystal]

It's not that you need your kids not to be energetic. You actually like that they have energy. You'll just like it even more when it's channeled toward doing their job and a little less toward annoying you until you're inches from your parental Bruce Banner impression...but still. You just need to help them learn how to expend their scientifically proven excesses of energy in a better direction.

Get him into sports. Which one? All of them. [Crystal]

Just Put Them in Sports, They Say

The most obvious answer you'll get if you ask a group of people how to channel your child's excess energy is going to be sports. Put them in sports! They'll go from whirling dervishes, hell-bent on destroying your home to exhausted, little angels in the span of one soccer practice. I find this to be less than likely for two reasons.

First, I've seen a Little League practice. It can't hold a candle to the amount of cardio my tiny terrors get in even the mildest game of hide and seek. There's no way a single sports practice is going to exhaust my kid into submission. I call BS.

Can we just put a junior crossfit in the backyard? [Crystal]

On top of that, if I were to put them in enough sports to actually exhaust them into sitting still, driving would be all I did, it would probably qualify as child abuse, and the subsequent exhaustion would not make them sit still but would more likely make them grumpy and miserable to live with.

Insert raised hand emoji here [Kristine]

---

52   Again, 100% true story. It was like a parental horror movie mashup of tap and parkour. *shudder*

53   Yet another true story. I swear the people at Nest cameras are going to send us a fruit basket one day with a note that says "just hang in there, champ...they'll grow up someday!".

Second, there is a logical fallacy inherent in the idea that sports will tire your kids out on a long-term basis. What using sports to try to exhaust your kids into submission will *actually* do is slowly train them into a higher level of cardiovascular endurance, making things oh so much worse on the days when they don't have practice. It's like using too much hand sanitizer and accidentally creating a super virus.

So, if the "just put them in sports" postulate doesn't pan out, how do you channel your kid's energy in a positive way?

Healthy Ways to Channel Unearthly Child Energy

There is no one way to do this, just like there is no one way to get a kid to eat their vegetables. Instead, I would like to put forth a list of suggestions. A menu, as it were, to give you a selection of different ways you can channel wall-banging, house-smashing maniacs into something more productive.

- Create a list of active, physically involved activities that your kids can do inside your house (without destroying it). There will be times when your kids have to let out steam when you can't take them to a secondary location. The larger your list of acceptable, in-home, roughhousing activities the more likely your kids are to be satisfied with ordering off the menu, so to speak. For example, I have a set of badminton rackets and a few birdies in our living room. This may sound like a shortcut to disaster, but if you actually examine a badminton birdie you'll find it is soft, squishy, and almost impossible to break a window with, even when hit at full speed. This is a great way for my 4-year-old to feel like she gets to hit something as hard as she can without wrecking the house.

  Oh man, the rackets would fly straight into our TV. [Kristine]

- Create safe zones without breakables, sharp corners, or really anything in them. You'll be shocked how much kids love a wide expanse of open rug. From sibling wrestling matches to unplanned cartwheels, kids just love a big empty space.[54] Having someplace you can release your kids from their "be careful" mandates and just let them run amok will release almost as much stress on your part as it does energy on theirs.

- Schedule bouts of activity before you want them to sit down. For example, I always try to plan to have my kids do something active right

---

54 There's so much room for activities!

before dinner. They stay out of my hair while I cook because they're off having fun (usually in a place in the house that's close enough for me to hear them but far enough that projectiles don't go in whatever I'm trying to cook), they come to dinner with at least the jagged edges worn off their energy, and they're a little extra hungry to boot.

- It is harder (not impossible, but harder) to move around while eating. If I make a rule that my toddler is allowed to eat a lollipop but only if she's sitting down, her little butt is uncharacteristically glued to the couch. It won't work for an indefinite period of time and it's not very healthy of a habit to do on the regular, but if you have a plane flight, wedding, or some other once in a blue type of event that really needs good behavior, some properly incentivized snacks (quiet, spill proof ones) might just help tip the scales in your favor.

- Put them in sports, just don't expect it to magically solve all your problems. There is a host of fantastic benefits kids get from sports, from leadership skills and teamwork to increased physical fitness and decreased risk of obesity. Sports are incredibly useful tools to further your kid's physical, emotional, and social development (Healthdirect, n.d.).

Cheat Sheet

Remember that kids physiologically have more energy and need less recovery time than you do. This doesn't help you keep them still, but it will help you not take it personally. You don't have demon spawn; you just have children. With this handy little science-fact in your pocket, you should be able to react to their random spikes of energy with a little more rationality and a little less "why are you out to ruin my life"-ism.

- Don't try to keep your kids from unstructured play. Remember that unstructured play has been scientifically shown to cause all kinds of fantastic learning and growth for kids (Milteer & Ginsburg, 2012), so don't try to stop your kids from running around the house screaming in fake French accents just because they look like tiny morons. They're actually learning important life lessons from the aforementioned moronic behavior.

- Try to attack specific bad behaviors rather than requesting complete stillness. Specifically, tell them to stop procrastinating, stop injuring your siblings, quit bumping the table while I'm trying to write, or quit making quacking noises in a demonic voice because you're scaring the crap out of the dog. "Sit still" is a tall ask, but it isn't unreasonable to demand they cease bad behaviors.

- Find healthy alternatives to get their yayas out. If you know your kids tend toward the energetic (read: if they moved any faster they'd be able to walk through solid matter), make sure they have enough opportunities to run around each day. This doesn't have to be sports, but it does have to be a daily (or more than that) time when they're allowed to run around like crazy people without consequences or reprimand.

12

Don't Watch TV

Intended Use: To get your progeny off their hindquarters and doing something productive with their lives

Possible Side Effects: Lower social competence, missed learning opportunities, definite eye rolling

This one is extra special because as often as we say it to our kids, I think we parents say it even more often to each other. Parents seem to love talking about the dangers of screen time, sharing diatribes against "the electronic babysitter," and making carefully worded snide comments about the superiority of parents who don't let their kids even walk into the same room as the dreaded, digital story box.

However, and I know this may be a minority opinion, I'm not entirely sure that television is entirely the enemy. I do agree that letting your child do literally nothing but watch YouTube videos in their darkened, cave of a bedroom is probably going to rot their brains and ruin their lives, but having some exposure to media, probably in increasing quantities as they get older, isn't actually as horrific a sin as some parents would lead you to believe.

In fact, if handled right, I even have some evidence that it can actually further your kid's learning in a good way. Also, having zero exposure to TV or other "screens" could also delay your kid's social development, deny them opportunity to gain necessary technological expertise, and give them a very different (and incorrect) picture of what the real world is like. While we will get to a section on "good TV," there are a lot of myths and fibs flying around about the infamous boob tube we need to handle before we get there.

Why We Say It

It's not hard to imagine why a parent would want to keep their kids from watching endless quantities of mindless television. Even though I do go through a few myths about the evils of television, I'll be the first one to admit that I'd rather my kiddos read a book, play outside, take a nap, or do almost anything else.[55]

You say this one because, as a parent, you see the TV colors flickering over your child's unblinking eyes and moronically gaping mouth, and you can just feel them getting dumber. Every parent on earth knows what I'm talking about. Kids don't just watch TV; they dive into it. We have literally played the game where we take turns saying our 4-year-old's name over and over in louder and louder voices to see just how loud we can get before she notices our existence over the allure of whatever low budget YouTube drivel is currently stealing her IQ points.[56]

While I'm definitely not making the argument that TV is good, I will categorize it as a necessary evil and show you the research on some very popular myths about TV and other media exposure so you can make an educated decision on what your kiddos watch and how much screen time they get.

Necessary evil. Some schools now use iPads instead of textbooks! [Kristine]

Research Says (What They Hear)

Alas, the war on children's media consumption has raged for a while now, but before I give you my personal take on it, let's go over some of the main battle lines that have been drawn.

Your Eyes Will Turn Square (and Other Myths)

Okay, so I must admit that my mom literally fooled me with this one when I was a child. I had apparently been watching TV all morning when my very humorous

---

55   Unless you ask me in the half hour in which I'm trying to cook dinner. In those 30 minutes I want them to kindly sit there quietly in front of the TV, rot their brains, and leave me alone to burn their chicken, unharrassed by questions about what kind of accent cows would have if they could talk.

56   The answer was uncomfortably loud (for us), but not 'sister took my snack' loud.

mom casually remarked that my eyes were starting to turn square, and my very worried, 5-year-old self sprinted into the bathroom to check in the mirror.[57]

The purpose of this story is not to illustrate how gullible I was as a child although I was exceedingly so but rather to illustrate that it has been multiple generations since moms began the anti-television crusade. In fact, I'm pretty sure cave women moms grunted angrily at their kids to stop watching the fire and to go outside and play with their dead squirrels.

Media and Violence

The overall sentiment of the public outcry on this one is simple: the more we let our kids watch violent television or play violent video games the more violent they themselves will be. Proponents of limiting violent media say that children model themselves after behavior they see on television and that the more kids see violence the more it will become normalized in their eyes.

While you clearly shouldn't feed kids (especially young ones) unmitigated acts of gratuitous violence in their TV, movie, or video game diets, there are also many instances where bad behavior generated by some other cause has been unjustly blamed on violence in the media. This is an incredibly complex issue with no clear-cut "right" answer, but there *are* some clear principles that can help you come to your own right answer for your family and your children.

> **Essential Note:** When it comes to advising, instructing, or judging *other* parents on how much television their kids should watch, I think I can safely speak on behalf of all parents when I say that we wish you wouldn't do that, regardless of your opinion on this or any topic.

Here are a few of the things you need to know to make an informed decision on what you do and do not let your kiddos watch on the violence front:

There Is No Single Cause for Violence

Whichever of the many sides of this issue you come down on, the first thing that everyone can probably agree on is that violence cannot be caused by one factor alone. Simply taking a nonviolent child and plunking them in front of a Quinten Tarantino marathon would not turn them into a violent sociopath no matter how many times you tried it.[58]

The way this is usually dealt with in the social sciences is through the biopsychosocial model initially proposed by a doctor named Applying this model to violence, (which has been done many times according to the literature on this topic

---

57   They were not, in fact, square.

58   This specific situation has not been tested by statistical research as I'm fairly sure there might be an ethical concern or seventeen somewhere in there.

(McKenry et al., 1995), means that in order for someone to become violent, that person usually needs a biological predisposition to violence, While this sounds like the most sadistic Wheel of Fortune puzzle ever, the premise is actually incredibly simple: patterns of bad behaviors, mental disorders, diseases, and other negative aspects of humanity are not caused by any one thing. Instead, everything has a biological component, a psychological component, and a social component. (Hence bio-psycho-social...duh...)

Applying this model to violence, (which has been done many times according to the literature on this topic (McKenry et al., 1995), means that in order for someone to become violent, that person usually needs a biological predisposition to violence, something to make them psychologically predisposed to act violently, and then a social trigger to set off specific acts of violence.

This means that a kid with no biological predisposition to act violently and nothing in their psychology to make them want to be violent would usually not resort to violence regardless of the social triggers such as seeing a graphically violent television show or playing a violent video game. (Read: if you aren't already aware of any violent urges in your child, your kiddo is probably safe whether you let them watch *Die Hard* with you on Christmas or not.[59]) Similarly a kid who was biologically or psychologically predisposed to violence could be protected if the right set of social circumstances (read: very good parenting, proper socialization, therapy, etc.) acts as a buffer.

However, if another kid *did* have a biological predisposition to violence and was *already* leaning in that direction psychologically, then a social trigger like a violent television show or video game could definitely tip the scales.

The take home message here is that if your kid shows no impulses toward violence other than the usual affinity to rough and tumble sibling play (and you would definitely know it if they did) and there is no history of violent behavior in your family (because many, though not all, biological predispositions are hereditary), then you probably don't have to worry that watching the occasional violent television show or playing the occasional graphic video game is going to set your kid up for a life of crime.

If you do see them starting to watch more and more violent stuff, beginning to exclusively prefer things with violence, or starting to act violently immediately following watching a violent TV show, you might want to start more carefully monitoring their media diet and definitely should begin having conversations with them about what they're watching.

Overall, most experts on the topic encourage parents not to immediately freak out about violence in the media, but rather to see it in the context of all the different influences on a kid's mental health (Black & Newman, 1995).

---

59   Because doesn't every American family watch *Die Hard* on Christmas? No? That's just us? Whoops.

Short-Term Effects of Seeing Violence

There are three basic psychological principles that you need to understand to judge the short-term effects of violence on your kiddos (Huesmann, 2007). These explain the instances in which your kids may act violently right after they watch something graphic on TV. Usually, the short-term effects go away as quickly as they appear, so this list is more of a parental list of why not to worry if your child momentarily appears to have turned into a sociopath.

Priming

Let's say when you and your spouse are getting ready together one morning you have a conversation about apples. Later that day, you find yourself having the apple walnut salad off the menu at lunch. You happen to make your kids apple slices with caramel as an after-school snack. Your spouse comes home with carry out apple pie for dessert as a family surprise. Is this a crazy coincidence? Not really. It's probably the work of priming.

Priming is a psychologically-demonstrated principle that when a concept is brought to mind once, the brain then shows increased reactivity to it when responding to subsequent stimuli (Hsu & Schütt, 2012). Basically, your conversation about apples that morning made both of your brains aware of apples. Then, whenever there was an apple-related choice to be made for the rest of the day, your brain said "hey, apples!" and went with that option. The priming effect wears off over time, so don't worry; you aren't doomed to a life of subconscious proclivity to Eve's favorite fruit.

The same thing happens when your children watch a violent TV show. What they're watching primes their brains to start thinking about violence so that when their sibling steals their snack,[60] their brain is more likely to yell "slap 'em!" than it would usually be. Priming is real, but it is only one of many forces so don't let your kid off too easy. Even a brain primed to violence doesn't erase the presence of their better angels, the rational control center in their brain, or the years of you shouting "don't hit your brother" at them.

Arousal

Before you start yelling at me for using the word "arousal" in a book about children, let me give you the disclaimer that "arousal" just refers to the state of having an increased alertness, attention, or interest (American Psychological Association, n.d.). Yes, the word is usually used to describe sexual arousal, but there is nothing inherently sexual about the term when used in a psychological context.[61]

---

60   Sliced up apples, of course.

61   So geez, get your mind out of the gutter.

When you talk about violent television causing psychological or physiological arousal, all it means is that sometimes your kid might see violence on TV and get pretty amped up. You've probably encountered a similar reaction when watching a violent movie that made you feel physically jittery or overly energetic. For the duration of my twenties (or at least until I started studying psychology), I used to come home from a scary or violent movie with the urge to go on a long run with no idea why.

My go-to is binge-cleaning. [Crystal]

It's not unusual for your kids to see something violent and display a greater level of arousal. Usually this just manifests itself in play-fighting, rough housing, or just jabbering at you with a nervous, excited energy to them. This is a completely normal response to seeing violence that can be traced back to the evolutionary likelihood that, if our caveman ancestors saw violence, it was likely they'd need to have more than the usual amount of energy to defend themselves against whatever was happening.

You don't need to worry about this type of response to violence unless it extends way after the initial hype has gone down.

Modeling

By far the easiest type of reaction to identify, modeling, is basically just your kid being a copycat.

One of the psychology experiments present in every intro psych class ever taught is one in which the famed psychologist Albert Bandura, father of social learning theory, let children watch a grown up play with one of those giant inflatable bobbly dolls that you can't knock down no matter how hard you try. Half of the kids saw the adult playing normally with the doll whereas the other half saw the adult basically beating the crap out of it.[62] As any parent can easily predict, the kids who saw the adult playing normally probably played normally as well, whereas those who saw the adult being unnecessarily and gratuitously violent toward the doll took it as an excuse to follow suit and beat the living tar out of the doll while yelling frighteningly creative insults at it.[63]

That is both alarming and sad! [Crystal]

The same can be said about children who start copying the behavior shown in a violent TV show or video game. We parents have seen our kids model everything from television characters, friends, family members, or even our own habits and actions.[64] Just like the phase where your child ran around scream-singing "Let It

---

62 In what I'm sure was the most fun job some psychology intern ever had.

63 This is actually true and one of the more alarming findings of the study.

64 This last one can either result in insanely heartwarming moments or spur guilty and troubled self-reflection on your part.

Go" after watching *Frozen* or wanted to march everywhere after watching the Von Trapp children get whistled at in *Sound of Music*, you can probably be pretty confident that any post-movie violent imitations should be similarly short-lived.

Long-Term Effects of Seeing Violence

While the short-term effects of seeing violence are usually small in consequence and go away as quickly as they came, the long-term effects of watching violence in the media are generally a little bit more worrisome. If you start to notice these manifesting in your kids, it might be time to start monitoring or limiting their exposure to certain programs, movies, or games, and it is definitely time to more carefully talk with them after they have watched something violent.

Observational Learning

Childhood is the time in which our small, developing humans learn what is and is not acceptable behavior in any given situation. It is for this reason that parents often sound like remedial tutors on human behavior for some alien species. No, on this planet it's not acceptable to run around the restaurant licking the top of each salt shaker. No, grabbing someone violently by the shoulders while screaming unintelligibly is not a socially accepted form of greeting.

Kids have just a short 18 years (and reasonably quite a bit less than that) to figure out how to act in each of the situations they'll be expected to participate in as adults. If you remember our discussion on schemas from back in Chapter 6, one of your kid's main jobs when it comes to learning to navigate the world is to develop a schema for each type of event. At a wedding, you dress up, sit still, and try to pretend it's not weird for a couple to make out in front of their entire family. At the park, you can scream and run around, but you still can't throw sand at other people.

Schemas are important because they help us know how to act even in a situation we've never encountered before. If you walked into a room where everyone was wearing black tie garb, you might not know what exactly the occasion was, but you could probably guess easily enough how you should behave.

The observational learning part comes into play because the way kids absorb these societal rules is by watching the actions of others. When your kids are infants and toddlers, these "others" are basically you and your spouse (or whatever network of trusted adults you have on your parenting squad rotation). As they get a little older, this circle slowly grows to involve siblings, teachers, peers, and a broader social network.

Unfortunately, our kids don't just get their input from the sources of which we approve, but also the things they see that we might not like so much, like television or other media. Just as the kids who saw the adult psychology intern beating the tar out of an inflatable doll were more likely to imitate their violent mannerisms, kids who repeatedly see scenes of violence might start to internalize the message that violence is an acceptable way to react in certain situations.

In their defense, a lot of this is correct. Superheroes often meet violence with violence, but I'd bet most parents would be okay with their child defending themselves even violently if faced with a supervillain.[65] The problem comes when they start internalizing the idea that violence is an acceptable action in situations where it really isn't.

Desensitization

Definitely the most talked about long-term potential consequence of exposure to violent media is the concept of desensitization. The basic idea of desensitization is that if a child is repeatedly exposed to images of violence (or sexual imagery or really any other form of negative visual input) they will slowly become less and less and less shocked by it (Huesmann, 2007). Then, when they are faced with violence, they no longer experience the fear, horror, anxiety, or repulsion that they otherwise would have felt, which hypothetically leaves them more free to plan out potential violent or aggressive actions without being hindered by those pesky negative emotions.

When you hear about violence in the media, usually by panicked or gaslighting newscasters trying to explain some horrific event, it's almost always about how seeing too much violence has made kids so desensitized to violence that they just did X, Y, or Z, and how horrible it is that their parents let it go this far.

While I am most certainly not saying I am going to single-handedly going to answer the debate over violence in the media, I can give you some statistics and facts that can help you decide what level of exposure is right for you and your kids:

- On average, US children watch between three and four hours of television each day (Comstock & Paik, 1991), and estimates show that 40% of these shows contain heavy violence (Wilson et al., 1997).

- 83% of households with kids have at least one video game unit (Roberts et al., 2005), and 94% of video games (at least those aimed at teens) are rated to contain some kind of violence (Haninger & Thompson, 2004).

- Across multiple studies, the correlations between exposure to violence in the media ranged from small to medium effect sizes, meaning there was a connection but it didn't pack a very big punch in terms of how much of a difference it actually made (Huesmann, 2007). However, studies that randomly separated kids into two groups and then showed one group violent television showed that exposure to violence created short term effects but no significant long-term effects.

---

65   For more on this, check out the chapter on "don't hit".

- Many researchers have suggested that instead of violent media making kids violent, that it may be the case that kids who choose to play violent games or watch violent television do so because they *already* have a predisposition toward violence so that's what they enjoy watching or playing.

Basically, there is solid evidence suggesting that violent media does have some effect on children but no evidence that seeing violence in media can by itself turn a nonviolent child into a violent criminal.[66] This means that it is a parent's job to monitor their child's media consumption, continually talk to their kid about what they're seeing on television, and be prepared to step in if they see their kid developing a greater than normal proclivity toward violent behavior.

Other (Just as Important) Considerations

While violence in the media gets far more attention than almost any other issue with children's programming, there are other things parents should consider when deciding what to let their kids watch. There is a lot of grey area in between a draconian television moratorium[67] and allowing your kid unfettered access to binge watch whatever strikes their fancy whenever they please. As with most things, the best answer involves moderation, forethought, and communication with your child.

When you're deciding what should and should not make the cut in your child's media diet, here are some things you should definitely consider.

Media and Gender Roles

Just a quick warning before we get into this one, standing on my "children's movies portray negative gender roles" soapbox is literally one of my favorite places on Earth.[68] I could write entire books on the damaging nature of the gender roles portrayed in children's TV and movies. I have taken entire courses on this subject. Literally. So, with that disclaimer, consider yourself warned, and let's begin...

It doesn't take a die-hard feminist to want to cringe when the Disney princesses of old are faced with a problem and dramatically throw themselves onto the nearest flat surface weeping hysterically. Similar to the weeping princess problem-solving strategy (or lack thereof), some of the negative gender roles portrayed by traditional children's programs are fairly easy to spot.

No parent is really that worried that their child is going to run away from home, abandon their family, borrow body-altering drugs from the neighborhood crack

---

66   You could most likely have guessed that about five pages ago, but now you at least have the statistics to back it up.

67   Say that ten times fast.

68   They say Disneyland is the happiest place on earth but standing on this particular soapbox is way more fun and way less expensive.

dealer, and move to a different country just because a man they saw once (but never actually spoke to) was handsome. That's why we still show our kids *The Little Mermaid*.

However, some other messages are a little sneakier and do actually permeate the mindsets of our kids. No one is worried that their child will fall in love with the violent criminal who once kept us captive (thanks, *Beauty and the Beast*), but the idea that someone can be mean, controlling, and threatening toward us and if we just keep being nice, kind, and trying to see the good inside of them they'll eventually turn into a good guy is equal parts plausible and dangerous.[69]

If children's TV stereotypes are to be believed, girls are fragile, fashion-obsessed, pink-wearing, purse-dog-carrying, poorly educated, lazy, egocentric narcissists that can't handle criticism, sports, polysyllabic words, or broken nails. And if you think boys get the better end of the stick, you would be incredibly wrong.

And are still somehow rescuers to our damsels in distress! [Crystal]

Boys are usually portrayed as clueless, emotionally-stunted, sports-obsessed troublemakers with a penchant for pranks, poop jokes, and avoiding any kind of hard work.

Yes, children's shows exaggerate for comedic effect. No, your perfectly normal she-toddler isn't going to turn into a fragile, shrill, egocentric fashionista just by watching one episode of *Barbie*.[70] However, no one who has seen a toddler watch television (usually involving both eyes wide open and their face a few inches from the screen) can deny that they are watching, learning, and modeling themselves after what they see on that screen.

Just like violence in the media, there is no one cause for gender inequality. However, it would be foolish to give our kids unlimited access to examples of magnetic characters peddling negative gender roles without thinking carefully about what they should and shouldn't be allowed to see, monitoring their access to things we deem to be past the line, and having serious, regular conversations to help them make sense of what they see.

Media and Stereotypes

While talking about negative gender stereotypes might be incredibly fun (at least to me), they are by no means the only negative stereotype being thrown at your kids every time they turn on the television.

There are negative stereotypes purveyed all over your kid's movies, television shows, video games, and other forms of media. There are harmful stereotypes about

---

69   And that, kids, is how abusive relationships are born.

70   But why risk it?

old people, gay people, overweight people, people from every different nationality or race, and almost every other marginalized group you can imagine.

Even more, there are negative messages for your kid about what the appropriate behavior is in a given situation. Movies subtly impart messages about all kinds of things. Siblings have to have rivalries and fight over toys. Old people are either caring grandparents or scary, grumpy villains. The protagonist of the story is always going to be thin and attractive. The list of negative messages that are subtly reinforced by your kid's steady television diet would shock and horrify you.

Other than banning your kids from any form of media (which is definitely unrealistic), there is no real way to prevent your kiddos from being exposed to these negative stereotypes. There is only the necessity for parents to maintain an active presence in their kids' media consumption and to have conversations that help your kids realize what is a stereotype for comedic effect or plot development and what is actually true.

The Portrayal of Villains

Before we move on, I promised in an earlier footnote that we would talk about one specific negative stereotype that I believe has an incredibly dangerous effect on kids: the way children's media portrays villains.

Think about your kids' favorite movies or television shows. Ninety-nine percent of the time, the villain is ugly, unrealistically thin or fat, and pale. They're often old and they almost always dress in black. Sometimes, as in the case of Ursula the sea witch[71] or Hades from *Hercules*, the villain can be spectacularly campy or have stereotypical homosexual mannerisms. As if all these clues weren't enough to clue you in that this character is up to no good, their arrival on screen is often heralded by some dark and creepy music.

This makes for very entertaining television, but the idea of setting our kids up with the idea that villains can be easily and immediately detected on sight is incredibly harmful. Not only does this paint a kind of grim picture for people who are old, ugly, like to wear black, or are unfortunate enough to have some other "villain-like" characteristic, but it also sets kids up with a very dangerous preconception: that the "bad guy" can be identified on sight.

True! Even toys have rough villains but clean-cut good guys. [Crystal]

If we let kids go into the world with the idea that they can visually determine who is good and bad, we are setting them up for a lifetime of disappointment (at best) and victimization (at worst). In real life, the creepy guy who's going to slip something in your drink at the bar looks just like the one who will walk you home

---

71   Ursula was actually designed after Divine, a man whom *People* magazine declared "Drag Queen of the Century". (https://www.sbs.com.au/topics/pride/fast-lane/article/2016/11/09/fun-fact-ursula-based-iconic-drag-queen-divine)

safely without even requesting a kiss. The girl who's going to try to steal things out of your dorm when you aren't there could be way prettier than one who will be a perfectly respectful roommate.

The idea that you can tell who a person is immediately or by the way they look is outright dangerous and needs to be combatted as early and often as possible. Kids need to be taught that a person's *actions* determine whether they are the bad guy or the good guy. They need to know that pretty people can be evil and that ugly, old, or otherwise "villain-looking" people can be immeasurably good.

So, while there are many different negative stereotypes, both about marginalized groups and about the acceptability of certain negative behaviors, if you do nothing else after this chapter please start talking to your kids about the fact that you can't tell if someone is bad or good until after you get to know them.

The Rise of YouTube

Finally, there is one more dangerous type of media that is currently on the rise: the ever present YouTube.

For those of you currently living under a very large rock, YouTube is a video sharing platform that currently brings parent company Google roughly $4 billion per year. If you want a reference point for just how massive YouTube has become, roughly 300 hours of content were uploaded every minute as of 2019. The highest paid YouTuber (who, ironically, is a 6-year-old boy) made $11 million in 2019.

I'm scared to see what becomes of that boy. [Kristine]

So yes, YouTube is massive, and a large part of the videos it houses are aimed directly at kids. My main problem with this isn't the predatory advertising that makes your child want every toy under the sun (even though it is and they do) but rather that it is contributing to the long-term degradation of the attention span of the American child.

To put this in perspective, the average children's movie is runs about 1 to 2 hours in length (Doctor Disney, n.d.), while the average YouTube video is 11.7 minutes long (Clement, 2019). At least a movie is teaching kids to sit down for a few hours straight, follow one cohesive plot from inception to completion, and cognize the comings and goings of one set of characters. When watching YouTube videos, everything is dumbed down to be easily-digestible in a matter of minutes. On top of that, your kid has the power to switch from video to video with ease, never developing the staying power to watch any of them through to the end.

I can't state strongly enough how much YouTube makes me worry for the developing attention spans of our kiddos. If you look up antonyms for "delayed gratification" in the thesaurus, you just see a picture of the YouTube logo.

As if this isn't bad enough, it's also accompanied by bright colors, high-pitched voices, flashing lights, annoying background music (60% of which is the same be-

Or some with beloved cartoon characters but pretty alarming narration. [Crystal]

cause many YouTubers use the same production software), less-than-educational plotlines, and sometimes shockingly low production value.

Together, all these things make me feel like we're diving a little too fast into the fictional world of *Idiocracy*, a 2006 documentary (oops, I mean comedy).

I'm fairly liberal with the screen time when it comes to movies or even television shows (as long as they're ones on our "okay" list), but if my 4-year-old watches too much YouTube, I can almost hear her poor neurons starting to die.

I'm not saying that there isn't a ridiculous quantity of really well-made, educational YouTube videos with helpful knowledge and thoughtful plots, but they are vastly outnumbered by the ones where they watch two siblings dress up as princesses, put on gaudy makeup, and shrilly fight over their age-inappropriate toys.

Yes, but those songs forever haunt my dreams...nightmares...whatever. [Kristine]

I think the best answer for YouTube videos is that they can be a great tool in very limited supply and with careful parental supervision, but that this is truly the shallowest end of the media gene pool and should be treated with the appropriate amount of caution.

Educational Television and Other "Good" TV

Some parents treat educational television like a myth, others like a get out of jail free card for letting their kiddos have unfettered screen time, and most something approaching careful skepticism. While there is some scientific evidence for the efficacy of educational television (Baydar et al., 2008), it also isn't a magic bullet or something that can substitute for actual interpersonal interaction or real life education.

I actually have a slightly snarky perspective on educational television, which is that all television is educational: they're learning something regardless of what they watch. That's why it's so important that you make sure your kids are watching things you have intentionally deemed appropriate. If they're watching kids pout dramatically and fight with their siblings, they're learning how to do that. If the characters are embodying crazy stereotypes, they're educating themselves to think along those lines. And yes, if the characters are speaking Spanish or talking about colors, they're learning that.

The problem with officially "educational" television is that it doesn't usually have the massive draw that mindless television has. Unfortunately, in order to learn things, your kid has to be paying attention. If you throw your child in front of educational television and they spend the entire time squirming and picking at their feet, they aren't absorbing the information. On the other hand, if you can get them to actually like a show that conveys helpful information (whether that be French, math facts, or the fact that girls can be as capable and powerful as boys), then they'll start internalizing that information as fast as they learned the chorus to "Let It Go."[72]

So, with that in mind, I'd say it's your job to find the television with the best messages you want to send your kids (whether it's television shows with good gender roles, movies that teach them about famous scientists, or the wonderful world of corny language immersion shows) and try to make them as fun and alluring as possible.

What to Say Instead

After all that we've talked about to do with different types of television, there is also the simple question of what the ramifications of just watching a screen in general. There has been a huge amount of research done in recent years on the effects of kids watching any kind of screen, be it tablets, smart phones, television, computer, or video game.

Overall, the prognosis is not great. Screen time has been linked to slower physical and cognitive development, obesity, depression, anxiety, and sleep problems (Domingues-Montari, 2017). Even more troubling, these effects are strongest when the screen they're watching is television (rather than something like a computer or video game that requires more interaction).

By now most clinicians have wised up to the obvious fact that it is impossible to keep kids away from screens entirely. I mean, even in school your kids are bound to watch some movies, spend time on computers, and even use iPads, depending on the district. However, there are some widely agreed-upon suggestions to limit kids' screen time and buffer them from the negative effects of the inevitable screen time in which they are bound to engage.

- Make a big push to limit screen time while eating. This promotes family connectedness at mealtime as well as encouraging healthier and more conscious eating behaviors.

- Don't put televisions in your kids' bedrooms. Having a TV in a child's bedroom has been linked to poor sleep habits, obesity, and even substance use. Also, it's easier to monitor what they're watching if all televisions are in public areas.

- Watch as much of your kid's screen time with them as possible. When parents and kids interact while watching media it turns it into more of a learning experience and mitigates the risk factors.

---

72   Okay maybe not quite that fast. *Nothing* happens as fast as children learn the lyrics to "Let It Go." Unfortunately.

- Really, please don't give kids under the age of two screen time. The significant negative impact of screen time on infants really isn't worth whatever benefit a few minutes of good behavior buys you as a parent.

Cheat Sheet

- Have your kids watch TV after they finish X, Y, or Z. Kids shouldn't come running home and immediately flip on the television. I know some people have this as an ingrained routine so it'll be hard to change up the habit, but try to channel your kids into something else before they get into TV mode. (This is because once you enter "TV mode," it's very hard to get back out.) If they're tired, have them lay down and read a book, if they're energetic let them play outside for a bit, but try to find some other way to decompress.

  TV on a weekday morning or after dinner never ends well. [Crystal]

- Don't watch too much TV. Television turns your brain off. Literally off. Your brain is more active when you're sleeping than when you're watching TV (Brain Performance Center Staff, n.d.). As is the case with most yummy things, some is okay but too much probably isn't good for you. TV is a great snack, but it shouldn't be your main course. Keep it limited to an hour or two a day.

- Don't watch TV while you eat. Being distracted while you eat leads to accidental overconsumption. (Oops, who ate my chips?) Teach your kiddos to interact with other human beings while they eat, then turn on the television later.

- Don't watch TV in your room (especially before bed). There are a vast number of studies documenting the horrible effects of television on your sleep patterns. TV can keep you from falling asleep, give you worse quality of sleep, and make you feel tired even though you did sleep. Preschoolers who watch TV actually sleep less than those who don't (University of Massachusetts at Amherst, 2019). And above all, falling asleep with the TV on can mess with your circadian rhythms, serve as a risk factor for obesity, and reduce the amount of restoration your body accomplishes during sleep, leading to decreased muscle healing and goes on (McKenzie, 2003).

- Watch TV with them. The best thing a parent can do to mitigate the risks of TV use is to watch it with their kid. Turning it into an interactive experience decreases the amount of "zoning out" brain inactivity, turns it into a learning and bonding experiences, ensures that you'll be able to talk about any concepts that need explaining or moderating (violence, stereotypes, sex, etc.), and limits the amount of television that gets watched.[73]

---

73   Because I'm betting you probably don't have all day to watch *Dora the Explorer*.

13

Clean Your Plate

Intended Use: To keep your kids alive
(on something other than ice cream)

Possible Side Effects: Poor eating habits,
unhealthy relationship to food, increased risk of
obesity, decreased enjoyment of healthy food

Alas, we finally get to the chapter for which this book was titled.

I didn't put this last because it was the most or least important (because I really don't think I could rank these statements if I tried) but because it was the inspiration for this book. So, it seemed only logical to use it to wrap up.

Now, let's get started with the thirteenth thing you say that's unwittingly ruining your kids' lives.

Why We Say It

You started cooking dinner at the usual time but your hellspawn was soooooooo hungry that you caved and made them a quick batch of microwave macaroni to hold them over until actual dinner was ready. They didn't eat the macaroni. You then served them actual dinner with the rest of the family, but they decided it was yucky and pushed it away with disgust. Now you're trying to eat while balancing a fussy baby on your lap, and you're starting to see red already. So, then when they ask for yogurt instead of dinner you cave in even quicker the second time in simple desperation to

Oh the age-old battle of not wanting them to starve... [Kristine]

just have them eat something so you can check off "feed the offspring" on your to do list and start the endless routine of showers and tears that will ultimately result in you getting to go to bed.

When they don't eat the yogurt, you are remotely possessed with the vengeful spirit of rejected dinners everywhere and you angrily inform your sulking progeny that they have to clean their plate or no dessert for them! Unfortunately, not only does this create some pretty bad eating habits over time and cultivate an entirely unhealthy relationship toward food, it also just plain doesn't work. As any parent who has been in this situation knows all too well, what follows isn't your offspring happily snarfing down their dinner (all three of them) in attempt to win their Oreos. No, in reality it's a horror film spinoff episode of *Shark Tank* in which your anger mounts as you haggle with an unreasonable toddler while suspenseful music plays in the background, trying to determine the magical number of bites they have to

On three different plates, because no two foods can touch. [Crystal]

eat before the nutritional powers that be are satisfied and they can just eat their dang Oreos in peace.

Once the words "clean your plate" are uttered, everyone has already officially lost. There are no winners when it comes to persuading unwilling kids to eat, only shades of losers. It sets you and your progeny at opposite sides of an avoidable standoff and leaves you little room to retreat without losing some serious face.

So, we will go on to talk about all the things that are wrong with this one, but in the end the most important reason you should stop saying this phrase is simply that it doesn't actually work.

Research Says (What They Hear)

This phrase makes perfect sense for a kid. Children's sole purpose[74] is to eat as high a ratio of unhealthy food as possible. Popsicles for breakfast? Let's do it. Skip dinner and go straight to cake? All over it. Follow their French fries with a chaser of potato chips? Way ahead of you. In fact, I've even successfully tricked my toddler

---

74   Other than annoying you into early senility, that is.

into eating healthy things just by telling her they were unhealthy; she wanted them on that fact alone before she'd even tried them.

Given your child's alternative function as a garbage disposal for fat-saturated, sugar-infused garbage, it only makes sense that you would want them to eat their fair share of healthy food before they begin burying themselves in chocolate cake. However, as you've seen with so many of the parental sayings in this book, what makes perfect sense when they're kids will translate into strange behaviors as adults.

My Freshman Fifteen (Because Freshman Seventy Doesn't Enunciate)

Every kid goes a little buck wild when they leave the protective cocoon of home for the first time.

While it normally involves unhealthy quantities of alcohol, I personally have the proclivity to party of a Tibetan monk so my "ragers" usually involved eating a large deep dish pizza by myself or beating four of my guy friends in a hamburger eating contest.[75] After performing a fairly impressive weight gain (for an aspiring sumo wrestler, not to mention a teenage female) in my first few years of college, I spent senior year learning to eat healthy, working out like my hair was on fire, and making a fragile acquaintance with the concept of moderation.

Now, I'm definitely not blaming my ridiculously irreverent college eating habits on the fact that my parents told me to clean my plate, but I will definitely attest to the fact that before I had to start thinking about health, fitness, and diets it never even occurred to me that I *shouldn't* finish my plate. Even now, as a normally-sized, thirty-something mother of three, I still have to regularly and intentionally remind myself to stop eating if I'm not hungry anymore.

Am I saying you shouldn't try to get your tiny humans to eat at least some of their dinner before they move on to eat (and probably wear) a terrifyingly large mountain of ice cream? Absolutely not. It's incredibly important for us parents to teach our kids to eat healthy food as our primary meal and to have unhealthy snacks as a sometimes treat afterward.

Clean Your Plate or No Dessert

Despite the necessity of getting your little monsters to eat, making dessert contingent on finishing their food conveys the hidden message that dessert is the prize and slogging through the healthy food is the dreaded task they have to complete before they get to said prize. This has a lot of things wrong with it.

First, your kids should be taught to enjoy all the food they eat. There is no good reason to put food in your mouth if you don't enjoy it. At that point you're just eating calories to eat calories, which isn't healthy in anyone's book.

If your kids really habitually doesn't enjoy their food, try getting creative. Have them help you pick out the menu for the week. Maybe let them help cook with you

---

75   Both of these stories are unfortunately true.

because we all know food is more fun when you are the one to prepare it (at least as a kid). You might have to do some work to get to this point but try to teach your kid that food should be enjoyable, not just something that is done to get to the better food.

Second, as an adult, the rule should usually be "eat until you're full," not "clean your plate." The clean your plate mantra is dangerous, especially now, because portion sizes have gotten so out of control. According to one study, portion sizes in America have grown exponentially in recent years. Between 1977 and 1996 hamburgers got 23% larger, snacks like individual bags of chips grew 60% larger, soft drinks got bigger by 52%, and the list goes on (McKenzie, 2003). While asking a child in the 1950's to clean their plate might have been reasonable, asking the same in 2020 could be tantamount to asking a 3-year-old to repark your car.

Before you ask, a different study reported that portion sizes affected how much people actually ate by a large margin. If people are given more food, they're usually going to eat it even if they don't want it. The clean your plate philosophy is still incredibly prevalent among adults. Why wouldn't it be? We establish our adult habits beginning in childhood. I still have to fight the urge to save the best bites of my meal for last (under the assumption that I'm definitely going to eat the whole thing) rather than eating the best parts first so I can stop when I'm not hungry anymore.

Don't inoculate your kiddos to follow this unhealthy pattern.

You can require that they eat a healthy portion or a serving size, but please don't teach them that they have to eat every morsel that is put in front of them.

What To Say Instead

I do want to make a note of the fact that toddlers and other small children have a weird relationship to food. Some kids are eating machines, some seem not to eat at all. I have one nephew who resists the first bite like his parents are using it to torture information out of him, but then once he's had the first bite he'll house the rest of the meal with a smile on his face.

The best toddler food advice I ever got was from our pediatrician. She is incredibly and reassuringly non-alarmist so, when we were grilling her on how to feed our newly-weaned baby, she gave us this sage advice: kids won't starve themselves. Give your kid a healthy meal. If they don't finish it, calmly help them put it in a "to go" box or Tupperware for later. Then, when they figure out their "dessert stomach" is still empty a few hours later they have no excuse not to get the healthy food back out and nom on that. This way they don't have to eat, but if they do eat it's guaranteed to be healthy food.

Mine loves asking for giant portions then becoming immediately full. [Crystal]

Cheat Sheet

- Eat until you aren't hungry. This should really be the litmus test for when a kid should stop eating. Bonus, if kids clamor for dessert, they obviously are still hungry and therefore still have some plate-finishing to do, at least until they aren't hungry anymore.

- Learn to enjoy healthy food. Your child might secretly (or not so secretly) desire to eat nothing but potato chips all day. Resist the urge to allow this. Try and find fun, healthy food choices. Maybe try something you can cook or bake together. Whatever it is, try to pique their interest in actually enjoyable healthy foods.

- Don't force it. If you make finishing their food a battle, the less they'll want to do it and the more miserable your nighttime meals would become. Use the to-go box strategy, and let it go.

- Takeout containers are your friends. Get to-go boxes for all your kids' meals, even the ones that are not really "leftoverable." Let your kids be hungry enough to motivate them to finish the most recently-saved dinner. Less waste, less hassle, total win.

Epilogue

I very narrowly avoided naming this chapter "So what the hell am I actually supposed to say as a parent?" but several early editors convinced me that it might be a little too long and too angry for a chapter title. I still disagree, but I yielded to my better angels.

I wanted to end the book with some overarching principles (there are seven of them) that came up in multiple chapters. Kind of an 'if all else fails' kind of thing that you can turn to in case of parenting emergency. These are not inviolable rules, but they are pretty good guidelines to help you navigate the intricacies of parenting.

As we saw in almost every chapter, there can be a huge difference between the words that come out of your mouth and the things your kids actually end up hearing. Unfortunately for us parents, what matters most isn't the words we use but the messages that get transmitted regardless of our language choices.

So, while I'm not about to tell you exactly what words to use,[76] if you do your best to impart these messages it's sure to help you raise balanced, rational, happy humans that will do good things for their world once you release them into the wild.

Principle #1: Scaffolding (i.e. Show, Help, Supervise)

This concept isn't actually mentioned by name in any of the chapters, but it's inherent in almost all of them.

Scaffolding is an educational practice for teaching kids how to do tasks of ascending difficulty with the ultimate goal of doing it by themselves. The technique

---

76 Though anything with four letters should be heavily considered with extreme caution. Your kids will throw it back at you with way too much joy.

basically boils down to the fact that you show a kid how to do something new (and slightly above their capability level), then you do it with them a few times, then you slowly remove your help until they are doing it themselves. The obvious metaphor of scaffolding comes in because scaffolding is necessary when a building is being built (and is less stable) but comes off when the finished product is ready to be revealed.

I love this technique because it helps guide parents as to how to teach kids new stuff and how to know whether we should help them along or back off and let the little monsters do it by themselves. When they first attempt a task above their capability level (which could be anything from tying their own shoes to doing an AP calculus proof to dealing with getting dumped) you first show them how to do it, then help a lot, then slowly offer less help, then you watch them do it by themselves.

As you can tell, inherent in the practice of scaffolding is the idea that they need to practice a new thing many, many times before doing it correctly, on their own, or (ideally) both. Use this as an opportunity to reinforce that failure isn't the end of the world, but simply a sign they haven't learned everything yet.

Use the concept of scaffolding as often as possible. We often expect our kids to see us do something once and immediately pick it up, but try to remind yourself that even the things that are easy to you (putting things away right side up or rinsing out your shampoo without accidentally waterboarding yourself) are not going to come automatically at first. It's our job to help them learn these things, even if they seem incredibly small, obvious, and/or moronic to us as (mostly) capable adults.

Principle #2: Childhood Is Practice for Adulthood

It's important to remember that the purpose of all the crazy things we do as parents is to create children who will be functional, happy adults. While on some days it really is a victory just to survive until bedtime, you should endeavor to keep the long-term goal in mind. It isn't about your kid acing their spelling test, dating the homecoming queen, or even getting into the best college. It's about creating an adult that will be able to live happily, on their own two feet, and who will become a productive and valuable member of society.

If you aim for and use this long-term goal as a litmus test for your parenting decisions in the short term, your moment-to-moment decisions will become much simpler.

Remember Neuroplasticity

Neuroplasticity is just the science-y way of saying that habits become ingrained the more you practice them.

This is incredibly relevant to parenting because, as the official CEOs of our kids' lives, we can forcibly ensure they're developing the right habits and, due to neuroplasticity, we can be pretty certain that these habits we intentionally install in our kids will persist long after they leave our domain.

If we consistently (and I do mean *every* time and without fail) make our kids brush their teeth as soon as they finish a meal, make their beds right after they get up, or shower right before they go to bed, they'll become adults who don't know why but really can't eat without brushing their teeth, who wouldn't even think of leaving the bed unmade in the morning, and who literally couldn't sleep if they wanted to unless they're freshly showered.

While this is fantastic for the physical habits you want them to develop, it's even more powerful when it comes to mental practices. If you take the time to teach your kid how to handle failure by using scaffolding techniques to analyze what went wrong, squeeze all the learning out of it, and then move on knowing it's not the end of the world, your kid will slowly but surely internalize these thoughts. If you do this as consistently as you make them brush their teeth, then you'll turn them into challenge-seeking optimists who aren't scared of or turned off at the concept of possible failure and who instinctively use their occasional failures to make themselves better.

The same goes for a million other parental concepts like teaching your kid how to act around people, how to relate to food, how to think about money, and more. The mental habits you install in your kids are just as, if not more, important than the physical ones. Thanks to neuroplasticity, they're just as permanent as well.

Teach Boundaries

Simply put, having boundaries means that you know your rights as a human being and you aren't afraid to do whatever needs to be done to ensure other people don't infringe on these basic rights. Your kids' basic rights include, but are by no means limited to, things like having control over their own body, who is allowed to touch it, and how they do so, knowing what they want and that they are allowed to have your own opinions even if they differ from those of someone they care about, and having a minimum standard of the politeness and respect with which they should be treated by anyone they come into contact with.

Hard for moms (aka jungle gyms) of small children to model... [Crystal]

Teaching your kids boundaries means that they leave your house not just knowing all of these things intellectually, but instinctively believing them because you've drilled it into their heads over and over. Not only do your kids have to know their boundaries but they also have to feel absolutely zero guilt about doing whatever they have to do to defend them. If you can do this successfully the payoff is huge.

Boundaries mean that when your kids' friends suggest that they try shoplifting, your kids shouldn't hem and haw. They shouldn't worry about the pros and cons of rejecting one of the "cool kids" or wonder if they could get away with it for the sake of their social lives. If you correctly teach boundaries, your kid will immediately and instinctively burst into laughter at the mere suggestion that they do something that's against their moral code, regardless of who's asking.

Boundaries mean if an adult or a peer tries to touch your kids in a way that makes them feel uncomfortable, they will have no hesitation to make the situation stop, whether it's via verbal objection, getting out of the situation, or by using the appropriate amount of physical force.

Boundaries don't come instinctively and it's often even more counterintuitive to try to defend them, but if you can drill your child's basic rights as a human into their thick heads by modeling how to defend them and giving them repeated opportunities to practice defending them on their own, you'll definitely have done a gold star job as a parent.

Principle #3: Build Skills, Not Achievements

As a parent, it's incredibly tempting to pursue outcomes. It is so easy to make things like getting straight A's, doing volunteer work every week, going to an Ivy League college, or even your kid's achievements after they enter the "real world" into reflections on us, how we did as a parent, how great of a job *our* kid is doing.

Don't fall for it.

Your job isn't to turn your kids into a perfect résumé. Your job is to give them skills. All the skills. A perfect set of achievements can always suffer a catastrophic failure, fall off their pedestal, or simply hit their peak too soon. If you turn your kids into a walking display case for the evidence of your awesome parenting, not only is there waaaaaaaay too much ego involved, but you are setting both of you up for disappointment.

Train your kids in life skills.

Instead of focusing on their perfect report card, work on creating kids who love learning and know how to self-diagnose when they haven't mastered something yet. Instead of getting them on the top club soccer team (or dance squad, or debate team, or whatever), focus on teaching your kid how to find things they are passionate about, how to balance their time between work and play, and how to be a productive member of a group.

The more you focus on skills the better off your kid will be in the long run. When your kid is 30, no one will care that the Little League team won state. They'll barely care what college your kid went to. (By 40, no one will even care about that.)

What *will* matter is that your kid is a person who knows how to learn new things, cares deeply about actions taken, knows how to self-improve, and (more important) has a way to determine what areas need improving.

Teach your kids skills and find something else to brag about at the PTA meeting. Your kid (and probably the PTA) will thank you later.

Principle #4: Embrace Failure As Your Friend

As you read in the love letter to failure in Chapter 2, failure is not only inevitable but incredibly necessary.

While you might be able to sneak by without failing in the academic world, the real world is not that kind of place. Failures are not only unavoidable in the real world, but you wouldn't want to avoid them because they are the primary way you learn anything of value.

Create as many opportunities as possible for your kids to fail. Teach them there's nothing to be afraid or ashamed of if they honestly try and honestly fail. Teach them to aim for challenging goals even when there's a risk that they'll fall flat on their face and put your money where your mouth is by being their biggest cheerleaders when they do. Showcase your failures with pride and let them watch as you pick yourself up, dust yourself off, curse a few times, and then use it to make yourself better. (This is the hardest, yet most potent way to drive the lesson home.)

Most important, when they do fail (and they will) you need to scaffold them through the process of failing productively. Over and over you should praise them for trying a hard thing, admit that not getting their desired outcome sucks, then help them diagnose what went wrong, figure out what they could have done better, help them make the necessary self-improvements, and then shove them back out there to try again as fast as you can. We as parents have an awesome power over whether our kids grow up to embrace challenges or flee at the mere hint of something hard. Use this power to create strong, resistant, failure-friendly kids.

Principle #5: Critical Thinking and Intrinsic Motivation Are The Holy Grail Of Parenting

The two most important traits for your kid to develop are critical thinking and intrinsic motivation.

If your kids can get truly, deeply, passionately excited about stuff and then think objectively and logically about whatever they're doing, I firmly believe that there's nothing they can't accomplish. Fortunately for us as parents, both of these qualities are modeled and taught (aka installed) in childhood.

To get kids intrinsically excited about the stuff they're doing, remember that autonomy, relatedness, competence, and purpose create intrinsic motivation. Find ways to make them feel like their activities are their own choice, tie things in to how they connect your kid with their greater social network or community, make them feel competent (even as they fail at things), and always remind them of the ways their current activities will enable them to accomplish their greater, long-term goals.

To get them thinking critically, there is no substitute for constant modeling and scaffolding. Ask them why things are the way they are. Help them respectfully question their surroundings, the people they interact with, and even their own predispositions. Kids are born curious, so do everything you can to encourage and further that curiosity.

If you can shape, model, and scaffold your kid to an intrinsically motivated critical thinker, you can be assured they're going to do some really cool things with their lives.

Principle #6: Get Your Kid Outside of Themselves

Children all begin with a very egocentric perspective. When you're a baby you are literally the only being that exists in your world, as a toddler the world exists to serve you, and then (after a brief break for elementary school) you somehow loop back around to that same misperception as a teenager.

Unfortunately, as adults, the world has repeatedly bashed us over the heads with the abundance of evidence that this couldn't be farther from the truth. The sooner your kids learn that the world around them is a big and diverse place that holds many people with their own lives, problems, perspectives, and desires (desires which have nothing to do with serving your child and their every whim) the better off they'll be.

Encourage a Larger Perspective

As soon as your kids are capable of verbal speech, start talking to them about things outside of themselves. As they eat dinner, open their thought to the idea that food they throw away uneaten could have been used to make another kid not go hungry. When they do their homework, don't let them skate by with the idea that the teacher just gave them homework to be mean. When you go to the park, have conversations about how strangers could be good guys or bad guys and that you can't

> *Or point out the homeless person on the way to dinner.* [Kristine]

know what a person is like until you get to know them. Every little seed you plant about how the world is large, complicated, and full of grey area will eventually come to fruition in the form of a more balanced, less selfish, and more self-aware child.

Encourage a Long-Term Perspective

Just as kids are born with the assumption that the world revolves around them, they also come with a very short-sighted view of things. Having a toddler think about something that happens five minutes into the future is a tremendous victory. Elementary schoolers are hard pressed to think about the next month.[77] Teenagers are so immersed in their own drama that it feels like the end of the world if something is going wrong with their wardrobe, hair, or social life.

Teach your kids that childhood is only a small fraction of their life as a whole, that their current problems will not be the death of them, and that everything is a small piece of a larger puzzle. Not everyone will be their friend, and that's okay. Boyfriends don't all turn into husbands.[78] Neither the relatives we love nor the ones we dread seeing will be here forever. The purpose of school is to prepare you for life not to get you into a good college. Most important, there will be a time when they pay all their own bills, do all their own laundry, try to civilize their own brood of kids, and look back at their childhood with desperate longing and jealousy of the simplicity of the lives led by their past selves. No effort spent trying to get your child to think in terms of the broader picture will ever be wasted.

Principle #7: Communication Is Key

Finally, I want to leave you with my final nugget of wisdom: talk to your kids.

No quantity of parenting books is ever going to give you all the answers. If for no other reason, this is because there is rarely a clear right or wrong answer in life.[79] There are always different perspectives to consider, different options to weigh, and an alarmingly large amount of grey area. So, talk to your kids about everything.

Entertain their stupid questions as toddlers and force them to continue talking to you as teenagers. Ask questions to get their points of view and actually explain your perspectives to them. Poke holes in their tiny world views and use scaffolding to talk them into more adult frames of mind.

> *So. Many. Questions. And yet, I hope he never stops asking them.* [Crystal]

Chances are your kid isn't going to be subtle about their needs, so if you are there and listening to them, it will be rare for a huge problem to catch you by surprise. When it does, you'll have established the communication channels to handle it together.

You'll never be able to parent perfectly all the time, but being there, present, and engaged with your child is all anyone can ever ask of you.

---

77   Unless it's their birthday, in which case they plan what feels like decades in advance.

78   Thank goodness!

79   In the immortal words of President Bartlet, those times almost always involve body counts.

References

Allen, J. (2019). Kidnapped children make headlines, but abduction is rare in U.S. *Reuters*. Retrieved October 27, 2020 from https://www.reuters.com/article/us-wisconsin-missinggirl-data/kidnapped-children-make-headlines-but-abduction-is-rare-in-u-s-idUSKCN1P52BJ.

American Psychological Association. (n.d.). Physiological arousal. *APA Dictionary of Psychology*. Retrieved November 3, 2020 from https://dictionary.apa.org/physiological-arousal.

Bagozzi, R.P. (!997). Goal-directed behaviors in marketing: the role of emotion, volition, and motivation. *Psychology & Marketing* 14(4): 309-313.

Baydar, N., Kagitcibasi, C., Kuntay, A.C., & Goksen, F. (2008). Effects of an educational television program on preschoolers: Variability in benefits. *Journal of Applied Developmental Psychology* 29(5): 349-360.

BBC. (n.d.). The Native American way of life and religion. Bitesize. Retrieved October 27, 2020 from https://www.bbc.co.uk/bitesize/guides/z3xftyc/revision/4.

Bettelheim, B. (1987). The importance of play. The Atlantic 259(3): 35-46.

Birat, A., Bourdier, P., Piponnier, E., Blazevich, A.J., Maciejewski, H., Duche, P., & Ratel, S. (2018). Metabolic and fatigue profiles are comparable between prepubertal children and well-trained adult endurance athletes, frontiers in physiology. Retrieved November 2, 2020 from https://www.frontiersin.org/ articles/10.3389/fphys.2018.00387/full.

Black, D., & Newman, M. (1995). Television violence and children. *British Medical Journal* 310(6975): 273-274.

Blatney, M., Jelinek, M., & Osecka, T. (2007). Assertive toddler, self-efficacious adult: Child temperament predicts personality over forty years. *Personality and Individual Differences* 43(8): 2127- 2136.

Brady, K. (2018, July 16). Is falling asleep with the TV on really that bad? *Health*. Retrieved November 3, 2020 from https://www.health.com/condition/sleep/falling-asleep-tv-on.

Brain Performance Center Staff. (n.d.). *Does TV rot your brain? Brain Performance Center* [blog].Retrieved November 3, 2020 from https://www.thebrainperformancecenter.com/rot-brain/.

Campbell, D.J. (2000). The proactive employee: Managing workplace initiative. *The Academy of Management Executive* 14(3), 52-66.

Chua, A. (2011). *Battle Hymn of the Tiger Mother*. London: Penguin Press.

Clement, J. (2019). Average YouTube video length 2018, by category. Statista. Retrieved November 3, 2020 from https://www.statista.com/statistics/1026923/youtube-video-category-average-length/.

Comstock G, & Paik H. (1991). Television and the American child. San Diego, CA: Academic Press.

Conroy, D.E., & Elliot, A.J. (2004). Fear of failure and achievement goals in sport: Addressing the issue of the chicken and the egg. *Anxiety, Stress & Coping* 17(3): 271-285.

DeDreu, C.K.W. (2007). The virtue and vice of workplace conflict: Food for (pessimistic) thought. *Journal of Organizational Behavior* 29(1): 5-18.

Deci, E.L, Koestner, R., Ryan, R.M. (1999). A meta-analytic review of experiments examining the effects of extrinsic rewards on intrinsic motivation. *Psychology Bulletin* 125: 627–668.

Deci, E. L., & Ryan, R.M. (1985). *Intrinsic motivation and self-determination in human behavior.* New York: Plenum.

Deci, E. L., & Ryan, R. M. (2012). Self-determination theory. In P.A.M. Van Lange, A.W. Kruglanski, & E.T. Higgins (Eds.), *Handbook of theories of social psychology* (pp. 416–436). Thousand Oaks, CA: Sage Publications Ltd.

Doctor Disney. (n.d.). Disney movies—list of years, running time, ratings. *Doctor Disney: The Ultimate Walt Disney World Study Guide.* Retrieved November 3, 2020 from https://doctordisney.com/disney-movies-list-of-years-running-time-ratings/.

Domingues-Montanari, S. (2017). Clinical and psychological effects of excessive screen time on children. *Journal of Pediatrics and Child Health* 53(3), 333-338.

Dweck, C.S. (2006). *Mindset: The new psychology of success.* New York: Random House.

Ekins, E. (2014). 57 percent of Americans say only kids who win should get trophies. *Reason-Rupe Poll.* Retrieved from https://reason.com/2014/08/19/57-percent-of-americans-say-only-kids-wh/.

Eliot, A.J., Dweck, C.S., & Yeager, D.S. (2005). *Handbook of competence and motivation.* New York: Guilford Press.

Engel, G.L. (1977). The need for a new medical model: A challenge for biomedicine. *Science* 196: 129- 136.

Gilovich, T., Medvec, V.H., & Savitsky, K. (2000). The spotlight effect in social judgment: An egocentric bias in estimates of the salience of one's own actions and appearance. *Journal of Personality and Social Psychology* 78(2): 211-222.

Graham, S., & Williams, C. (2009). An attributional approach to motivation in school. In K.R. Wentzel & A. Wigfield (Eds.), *Handbook of motivation at school* (pp. S 11–33). New York: Routledge.

Grusec, J.E. (1992). Social Learning Theory and developmental psychology: The legacies of Robert Sears and Albert Bandura. *Developmental Psychology* 28(5): 776-786.

Gunders, D. (2017). Wasted: How America is losing up to 40 percent of its food from farm to fork to landfill. *NRDC [National Resources Defense Council].* Retrieved October 27, 2020 from https://www.nrdc.org/resources/wasted-how-america-losing-40-percent-its-food-farm-fork-landfill.

Hales, C.M., Carroll, M.D., Fryar, C.D., & Ogden, C.L. (2017). Prevalence of Obesity Among Adults and Youth: United States, 2015–2016. *NCHS Data Brief* 288: 1-8. Retrieved November 2, 2020 from https://www.cdc.gov/obesity/data/childhood.html 79 Heck or just into the front yard to experiment with breath.

Haninger, K., & Thompson, K.M. (2004, February 18). Content and ratings of teen-rated video games. *JAMA* 291(7):856-65.

Healthdirect Staff. (n.d.). Developing life skills through sports. *Healthdirect.* Retrieved November 4, 2020 from https://www.healthdirect.gov.au/developing-life-skills-through-sports#:~:text=Physical%20activity%20has%20been%20shown,and%20self%2Desteem%20in%20children.

Huesmann, L.R. (2007). The impact of electronic media violence: Scientific theory and research. *Journal of Adolescent Health* 41(6 Suppl. 1): 6-13. 102.

Hsu, N., & Schütt, Z. (2012). *Psychology of priming (Perspectives on cognitive psychology).* Hauppauge, N.Y.: Nova Science.

Karpicke, J.D., & Roediger, H.L. (2006). Repeated retrieval during learning is the key to long-term retention. *Journal of Memory and Language* 57: 151-162.

Knittel, M.G. (2017). Why is it important to have personal boundaries? *Psychology Today.* Retrieved September 2, 2020 from https://www.psychologytoday.com/us/blog/how-help-friend/201711/why-is-it-important-havepersonal-boundaries.

McChesney, C., Covey, S., & Huling, J. (2016). *The 4 Disciplines of Execution: Achieving Your Wildly Important Goals.* New York: Free Press.

McKenry, P.C., Julian, T.W., & Gavazzi, S.M. (1995). Toward a biopsychosocial model of domestic violence. *Journal of Marriage & Family* 57: 307-320.

McKenzie, J. (2003, January 21). Food portion sizes have grown—a lot. *ABC News*. Retrieved November 3, 2020 from https://abcnews.go.com/WN/food-portion-sizes-grown-lot/story?id=129685.

Milteer, R. M., & Ginsburg, K. R. (2012). The importance of play in promoting healthy child development and maintaining strong parent-child Bbond: Focus on children in poverty. *American Academy of Pediatrics* 129(1): e204-e213.

Newsweek Special Edition. (2015). Michael Jordan didn't make varsity—at first. *Newsweek*. Retrieved October 27, 2020 from https://www.newsweek.com/missing-cut-382954.

Ramsey, D. (n.d.). Tithes and offerings: Your questions answered. *Ramsey*. Retrieved October 26, 2020 from https://www.daveramsey.com/blog/daves-advice-on-tithing-and-giving.

Roberts, D.F., Foehr, U.G., & Rideout, V.J. (2005). *Generation M: Media in the lives of 8–18 year- olds*. Menlo Park, CA: The Henry J. Kaiser Family Foundation.

Rowling, J.K. (2008). The fringe benefits of failure and the importance of imagination. *The Harvard Gazette*. Retrieved October 27, 2020 from https://news.harvard.edu/gazette/story/2008/06/text-of-j-k-rowling-speech/.

Ryan, R.M., & Deci, E.L. (2017). Self-determination theory: Basic psychological needs in motivation, development, and wellness. New York: Guilford Press.

"Sam". (n.d.). The average percent of income donated to charity. Financial Samurai. Retrieved October 26, 2020 from https://www.financialsamurai.com/the-average-percent-of-income-donated-to-charity/.

Torney-Purta, J. (1991). Schema Theory and cognitive psychology: Implications for social studies. *Theory and Research in Social Education* 19(2): 189-210.

University of Massachusetts at Amerherst. (2019, May 14.) Preschoolers who watch TV sleep less. *Science Daily*. Retrieved November 3, 2020 from https://www.sciencedaily.com/releases/2019/05/190514110316.htm.

Wallace, J.B. (2015). Why children need chores. *Wall Street Journal*. Retrieved October 26, 2020 from https://www.wsj.com/articles/why-children-need-chores-1426262655.

Whitebread, D., Basilio, M., Kuvalja, M., & Verma, M. (2012). The importance of play. *Toy Industries of Europe* 4: 1-55.

Williams, R.L. & Worth, S.L. (2001). The relationship of critical thinking to success in college. *Inquiry: Critical Thinking Across the Disciplines* 21(1): 5-16.

Wilson B.J, Kunkel, D, Linz, D, Potter, J, & Donnerstein E., Smith, S.L., Blmenthal, E., & Gray, T. (1997). Violence in television programming over-all: University of California, Santa Barbara study. In M. Seawall, Ed., National Television Violence Study. Vol. 1 (pp, 3-184). Thousand Oaks, CA: Sage Publications.

Zivkovic, S. (2016). A model of critical thinking as an important attribute for success in the 21st century. *Procedia Social and Behavioral Sciences* 232: 102-108.

Select MSI Books

Parenting

10 Quick Homework Tips (McKinley Alder & Trombly)

108 Yoga and Self-Care Practices for Busy Mamas (Gentile)

365 Teacher Secrets for Parents (McKinely Alder & Trombly)

Choice and Structure for Children with Autism (McNeil)

Courageous Parenting (Omer)

Girl, You Got This! A Fitness Trainer's Personal Strategies for Success Transitioning into Motherhood (Renz)

How to Be a Good Mommy When You're Sick (Graves)

Lessons of Labor (Aziz)

Life after Losing a Child (Young & Romer)

Mommy Poisoned Our House Guest (S. Leaver)

Noah's New Puppy (Rice & Henderson)

One Simple Text... (Shaw & Brown)

Parenting in a Pandemic (Bayardelle)

Soccer Is Fun without Parents (Jonas)

Understanding the Challenge of "No" for Children with Autism (McNeil)

Our Pandemic Series
Books by Experts to Manage the Pandemic

10 Quick Homework Tips (Alder & Trombly)

Choice and Structure for Children with Autism (McNeil)

Diary of an RVer during Quarantine (MacDonald)

Exercising in a Pandemic (Young)

God Speaks into Darkness (Easterling)

How to Stay Calm in Chaos (Gentile)

Old and On Hold (Cooper)

Parenting in a Pandemic (Bayardelle)

Porn and the Pandemic (Shea)

Seeking Balance in an Unbalanced Time (Greenebaum)